Freedom

And

Opportunity

Stop
Redistributing
and Downsizing
America

Wayne L Staley

MISSION

The purpose of this book is to act as a catalyst towards developing a national mission statement and shared agenda based on freedom, opportunities, and a free-market system. To compete in the global arena, America must be a self-sustainable nation built on equality, environmental integrity, entrepreneurship, advanced technologies, a first class education system, leading edge health care system, and moral human principles. We must build a powerful economy, strong military, and return to the rule of law.

Cover, photography and Graphics by:

Phase Four Graphics LLC

Copyright © 2014 by *AFFINITY SYSTEMS LLC*

ISBN-13: 978-1503347434
ISBN-10: 1503347435

DEDICATIONS

This book recognizes the fragility of liberty and opportunities for all future generations of Americans.

I salute my brothers and sisters in arms, past present and future, serving to preserve the democracies of this great American experiment. Our work continues, but it takes a different form, to speak clearly against any person or organization attempting to harm our liberties.

Memorial from Gettysburg National Cemetery

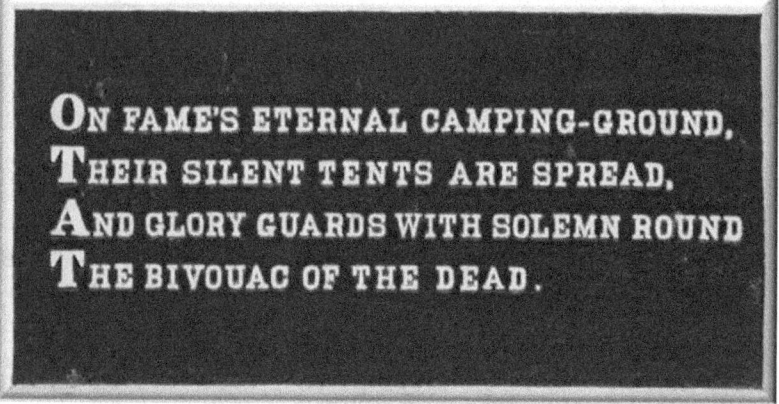

On FAME'S ETERNAL CAMPING-GROUND,
THEIR SILENT TENTS ARE SPREAD,
AND GLORY GUARDS WITH SOLEMN ROUND
THE BIVOUAC OF THE DEAD.

Theodore O'Hara

Recognition of service extends to law enforcement, firefighters, and other emergency personnel, working continuously, often under duress or in danger to keep us safe.

America has provided unparalleled opportunities to the world, but today, entrepreneurial America is under attack. Our children and grandchildren, regardless of gender, race, or religion, need opportunities enabling positive futures. We need to regenerate a competitive America, one capable of sustaining future generations.

ACKNOWLEDGEMENTS

The one constant source of support is Natalie Groshek Staley, my wife partner and my best friend in life. Thank you.

TABLE OF CONTENTS

Mission II
Dedications IV
Acknowledgements V
Table of Contents VI
Introduction VII

Religious Freedoms 1
Equality 10
The Wasp in the Window 17
Sharpen the Focus on Business Fundamentals 21
Chickens 24
Poverty Hurts 24/7 26
Why? 32
Defining Quality 40
Do the Means Justify the End? 48
Happy Mother's Day 56
Trust 60
Our Turn 69
The Children Immigrants 79
Of Cows and Cattle 91
Coming Soon - A National Data Base of You 95
The Redistribution of America 114
Your Choice - Policy or Opportunity Driven Society 136
The Zone of Opportunity 149

About the Author 162
Bibliography 168

INTRODUCTION

America has more resources than any country on earth. We can lead a Fourth Industrial Revolution, fueled by a reconfigured energy base, applied technologies, entrepreneurship, and pragmatic ecological perspectives. That includes buying products from countries and producers who meet the environmental expectations of our society. We now purchase cheap products from China, the single largest polluter on earth, while they avoid the penalty of clean energy. This double standard severely penalizes the American economy, restricting opportunities for our citizens.

Compounding the situation, our Federal government, under the guidance of the Obama Administration, has taken numerous actions to downsize and redistribute America. These actions are unilateral, punishing, and they restrict commerce in America.

The fundamental dilemma is that we have drifted away from the principles that made us an economic power, and are trying to find the appropriate balance with social and environmental imperatives.

For eighteen months, our Focused Fire Newsletters have researched the problems blocking the way for an opportunity driven society, a more successful economic model. We compiled the newsletters into one manuscript and added epilogues to selective issues, then summarized the challenges in The Zone of Opportunity.

Most Americans want the same basic outcomes. They want a strong economy, good jobs, a clean environment, responsible government, viable education system, and reasonably priced health care. All are part of the American dream.

God gave America abundant resources; we must be good stewards and not bury our talents. It is our choice.

RELIGIOUS FREEDOMS

June 2013, Issue 1

Freedom is the essence of America, cast into the foundation of the Republic by the Framers, and locked into the Constitution and Bill of Rights. The Constitution guarantees the fundamental rights of life, liberty and the pursuit of happiness. The Bill of Rights extends the list, including freedom of religion, speech, press, assembly, and the right to petition the government. Multiple rights are under assault by the Obama administration, but this paper's focus is on religion.

Religious Freedom

Religious freedom is the core premise of the United States of America, the shining light to the politically and religiously persecuted since the pilgrims stepped on Plymouth Rock. The religious composition of the founding fathers included Episcopalian, Anglican, Congregationalist, Presbyterian, Quaker, Unitarian, Catholic, and Deist.

The current religious mix of the United States shows 83% of the population with some type of affiliation, roughly 16% unaffiliated, and 1% unknown. The two largest groups are Christian. Protestant, with a varied makeup, represents 51%, and Catholic is 24%. Of these other religions, Jewish, Buddhist, Muslim, and Hindu are less than 2% per category. (*Source: Pew Forum on Religion & Public Life / U.S. Religious Landscape Survey*).

Why is a website dedicated to American Competitiveness writing a paper on religious freedom? Simple - business does not operate within a vacuum. The constitutional freedoms making Americans the most successful people in history are the same ones driving our economic activity. When government has the power to control religion, it can control the people, production, and distribution systems just as easily.

Some people foolishly want to make this a Democrat or Republican issue. In fact, it lies at the foundation of who we are as people. A loss of freedom will affect every person currently and all future generations. We may become one people again, without a party affiliation, and without a choice.

A government pushing the boundaries to gain power has little concern for color, religion, and social class, other than how to manipulate groups to achieve their purpose. Citizens must remember that centralized authority is antithetical to freedom.

The Catalyst

President Barack Obama, under authority granted by his Affordable Care Act (ACA), ordered the Catholic Church to violate core church values. Catholic theology states that humans do not have the right to block conception, and that once conception occurs aborting the child is murder. The administration forced a confrontation by demanding that the Church and affiliates offer coverage for birth control and morning-after pills, which are abortifacients. Faced with a firestorm of dissent, the Obama administration backed off partially, exempting the Churches, but not the affiliates such as the hospitals and charities. Backing further away, Obama agreed to have the birth control and morning-after pills paid for by the insurance companies. The problem is that many of the affiliates are self-insured.

In this situation, the Catholic Church has four options. One, ignore the order, with all the legal ramifications; two, comply with the order and violate church doctrine; three, disband the charities and hospitals; four, discontinue all health care insurance and pay the penalty. This throws all the workers onto the newly established health care exchanges, when they are completed. To avoid an election confrontation, Obama delayed implementation for one year, and that year is nearly over.

Many think this is a women's rights issue. The majority of younger Catholic women use birth control, and coverage is included in 80% of the health care plans. Women without coverage typically pay $20 to $50 dollars a month for birth control. (Source: Costhelper.com). While the ACA provides significant and important benefits, the services are not free and insurance premiums will rise to absorb the cost. (Source: Jodi Jacobson, Editor-in-Chief/RH RealityCheck, expert on women's health and rights). It also raises another question, would most women sell religious freedom for $240-600 year, especially when the insurance rate increases by at least that amount?

Actually, this is a religious and women's rights issue. The Church cannot both buckle and retain its doctrine. In either case, the Obama administration has created a paradox for employees of Catholic organizations. If organizations disband, there will be wholesale job losses and women's services provided by Catholic organizations will stop. If employers drop the insurance coverage, employees, many of them women, will have to deal with the exchanges.

A harbinger of future consequences has already occurred. The Catholic Church is unwilling to bend on the doctrine that marriage is between a man and women. They are shutting down adoption centers rather than place children with same sex couples. In point, there are enough

3

agencies that none has to be everything to everyone. Sadly, people caught in the controversy have lost their jobs.

The Affordable Health Care Act will radically affect every American. The research my co-author and I did for our book, "Crunch Time for Health Care," clearly indicates that health care costs, already out of control, are going to escalate. At the same time, services will suffer. The reason the Obama administration focused on Health Care is obvious. If government has control over medical care, it increases control over the people. Women's health is a straw man to draw attention from the damage it will eventually cause to families. The administration delayed the implementation until the election is over. Starting in October 2013, people will discover how much it really costs and how it will change their lives.

In the final analysis, it appears the Obama administration would celebrate the disintegration of the Catholic Church and all religious organizations. Advocates of big government see religion as a threat, and in nearly every historical case, government has attempted to eliminate or mitigate power threats. The key exception is atheism, which is often an ally of elitism.

Religious Rights

This brings us to the point. Americans enjoy religious rights like few other countries in the world. It is this right that makes us great. It is a joy to drive down a highway and see a cross, a minaret, or a country church with a steeple.

I listened to the emotional power of the Baptist music that buoyed Martin Luther King and the black community, as they fought for equality. The music of the Protestant reformation inspires me, and Jewish music causes longing for moments lost in time. The Islamic call to prayer reminds that diversity enriches us all. Attending a Latino Mass at Our Lady of the Valley Church in California, with the rich music sung in Spanish, is a great joy. Religion helps us deal with death and sorrow; it comforts us when things go wrong. Religion lifts and enriches us as one people, under God, giving us moral purpose beyond ourselves.

This election (2012) may have determined the fundamental right to worship as we please. President Obama demonstrated his contempt for religion in multiple ways.

First, President Obama disrespected his pastor, Jeremiah Wright, when their friendship caused unfavorable press reports. While not a believer in Black Liberation Theology, I respect the right of all people to practice their own religion. Jeremiah Wright was a Marine, who served his

5

country. I was an Army medic; therefore, Jeremiah Wright is my brother in arms, and I would choose him unequivocally over Barack Obama to cover my back. We have paid the price for the right to free speech, freedom of religion and total equality.

The second and third insights on the issue of freedom of religion occurred during the Democratic National Convention. The platform omitted any mention of God, or references to Jerusalem as the Capital of Israel. The subsequent uproar resulted in the reinstatement of both by a mock two-thirds vote.

The message was very clear on both points. In the past, the Democratic platform has shown contempt for the Jewish state, and the platform reinforced that obvious conclusion. The Obama administration appears to reject religion of every type, except for Islam.

In Conclusion

It is time to return to facts and reality, not the smoke and mirrors used by the Obama machine to cloud the issue.

Attempts to force the Catholic Church to violate its fundamental doctrines are in process.

The Democratic Convention platform omitted the word "God."

The Obama administration failed to recognize the sovereign boundaries of Israel.

The Obama administration omitted Jerusalem as the Israeli capital in the Democratic Convention platform.

Pres. Obama threw Jeremiah Wright under the bus when he became "inconvenient."

These facts are hard. The Obama administration has opposed religion at every step, except for Islam; therefore, one must conclude that if Barack

Obama has the opportunity, he will eliminate the core premise of America, religious freedom. This is the new REALITY!

If the persecution of the Catholic Church is successful, personal freedoms will significantly erode, negatively affecting all faiths without exception. All religious faiths enjoy equal rights under the law, and every American has the right to worship without government interference. Citizens should not have to go to bed at night and pray for their right to worship.

It gets worse. He will probably appoint two or more Supreme Court Justices, and religious freedom will move from jeopardy to history. It will be a dark, cold world without respite.

This is an American, not a Democrat or Republican issue. Twenty years in the future, no one will care about labels. Our children and grandchildren will be justified in asking, "How could you have been so stupid, selling us into government-controlled serfdom?"

I have always believed in the incredible judgment of the American people to change destiny. The 2012 election shook that belief to the core. The people made a choice negatively affecting every citizen.

The Rev. Jeremiah Wright made the comment, "The chickens will come home to roost." Although he referenced a different context, in President Obama's case, the true character of the man is coming into focus, and the chickens are flying into the coop.

A free America, filled with opportunities, will release the pent-up power of the entrepreneurs, lifting everyone. A large centralized government destroying the foundation of our Republic takes everyone down.

It is never too late when free people wake up, understand the threat, and take action. There is not much time left. Before the end of 2013, we will continue to be free people, or on the slippery slope to a dystopian state. Without religious freedoms, there cannot be a free, competitive America.

Epilogue

Religious freedoms

The Little Sisters of the Poor, a Catholic religious order servicing the poor and elderly, continues to be a target for the Obama administration in spite of a Supreme Court ruling.

> "In a one-page order issued by the court without any noted dissent, the justices said that — at least for now — the Little Sisters of the Poor did not have to follow the procedure the Obama Administration established for religious groups to escape complying with ACA-related rules requiring that employer-provided coverage includes contraceptives.
>
> Instead of filling out a government-issued form, the nuns can simply send the Department of Health and Human Services a written notice that the order is an organization with "religious objections to providing coverage for contraceptive services."
>
> http://www.politico.com/story/2014/01/contraceptive-mandate-obamacare-little-sisters-for-the-poor-supreme-court-102587.html

The Obama administration has rewritten the rules in an attempt to circumvent the Supreme Court.

The battle over religious freedoms in America has moved through the courts, with an uncertain future. Throughout history, the citizens counted on the Supreme Court to support our freedoms, but like the rest of government, it has become timid and unpredictable.

Obama and Israel

America and Israel have enjoyed a strong relationship since its establishment in 1948 as an independent country. Nearly from the first-day President Obama took office, his outreach has been to the Islamic world, which he supports with words and actions, frequently at the detriment of our relationship with Israel.

Recently, a White House staff member used a derogatory expletive referring to Prime Minister Benjamin Netanyahu. In essence, accusing him of lacking the courage to attack Iran and destroy their nuclear weapon potential. The hypocrisy was that prior to the 2012 election, the administration, concerned that Netanyahu would attack Iran and negatively affect election results, leaned on Netanyahu, forcing him to back off.

Benjamin Netanyahu is a decorated warrior, his bravery proven in numerous conflicts. He is therefore a brother-in-arms in the war against tyranny. It is laughable when spineless bureaucrats without military experience accuse a war hero of cowardly actions.

President Obama is pursuing an arm's agreement with Iran, a country vowing to replace the government in Israel. (There is a controversy over the interpretation for the phrase then Iranian President Mahmoud Ahmadinejad used, but the meaning is clear, the elimination of the nation of Israel as a democratic Jewish state). If Iran develops an atomic bomb, the world will instantly become a far more dangerous place, putting Israel and America in imminent danger.

America has few friends in the Middle East, and it is suicidal to embrace our enemies while throwing friends under the bus. We must judge only actions when the intent is unknown. Something, however, is going on that we are unaware exists - a huge political, secret iceberg buried under the opaque sea of our ignorance, further concealed by the absence of government transparency.

EQUALITY

July 2013, Issue 2

The joy about being an American is in having the freedom to write anything. We sit behind our desks surrounded by comfortable objects. Facts to support our opinion are available via the Internet, and picked to support starting premises. Liberals and conservatives alike participate, often in stereotypical terms, in the dance of lies and misinformation, in the name of "intellectual honesty." Fired into cyberspace, these missives have little accountability and lack bias checking by peers.

Affinity Systems LLC is a consulting firm, and our new model is research and publications. Our skills are manufacturing, computer systems, quality, and Lean Six Sigma. Our work applies systems and thinking tools to analyze complicated systems - structures of all types. Action starts by identifying root causes through a process separating symptoms from problems, distortions from reality, then defining solutions for the problems. Once implemented, solutions must meet or exceed our customers and our own standards. There is no place to hide. We live by the merits of our work. Our mantra is to find and understand the facts to arrive at the truth within our scope of reality.

Having grown up in southern Kansas in the 1950s, I have personal experiences with deep-rooted cultural prejudice. Oklahoma, five miles south, had "blacks" and "whites" rest room facilities and water fountains. There was an Indian school, where children ripped from their tribal parents, received programming to think like whites. My hometown had separate swimming pools and seating sections in the theatre. Our family was poor and lived in a racially mixed neighborhood. I have seen, felt and been guilty of prejudice. It is easy to blame poverty, but prejudice extends to wealth, status, religion, nationality, sex, and sexual orientation.

As an adult living in Milwaukee, I witnessed prejudicial conditions where anger manifested itself in multiple, different ways. There were racial riots and protest marches on the streets. I learned how to deal with prejudice from a very intelligent friend, a system analyst working for IBM. We were on an elevator, with demonstrations taking place on the streets below. The message was "Never group people. You must understand situations one person at a time, then as individuals within groups."

My friend was female, black, and right.

Reducing the human value makes it easier to subjugate people, and prejudice is not limited to race or social status. When I was a child, many Americans held Jews in contempt. In Nazi Germany, Joseph Goebbels, master propagandist, turned on the social programming machine. One of his tools was stereotyping. When an individual or group of humans can be "put in their place" through lumping into extreme categories, they are more easily mentally, then physically enslaved. A programmed populace looks the other way, just as the Germans did during the Holocaust and whites when blacks were enslaved. While these are both prime examples, the Native Americans suffered brutally under a policy of governmental genocide, accentuated by General Sheridan, "The only good Indians I ever saw were dead." In the West, shanghaied Chinese immigrants were literally beasts of burden.

Recently, I received a justification for why conservatives are misguided. The writer quoted materials proving conservatives are less educated, ignore the lessons of science, and harbor greater prejudices against literally "everyone else." It painted the extremes in broad generalities to justify the "analysis." Joseph Goebbels would love the matrix. The word conservative is interchangeable with Christian, Muslim, Jew, and Black, Red, liberal, rich, poor, men, women or any other group. Changing the metrics reflects the correct stereotype.

It is my sincerest hope that Americans get off this stereotyping kick of liberals and conservatives, or identifying Americans by race. We are all colors, all opinions, and all faiths. Collectively, we sparkle like gold. My mantra is freedom. Slavery equates to a lack of freedom. It means that someone or a group of persons is attempting to control what and how we think and act. Our government, in this context, is the major offender, and working hard to keep us from unifying. Discernible people recognize the difference between verbiage and reality. They park their computers and go find out what is happening. Even as we argue against traditional forms of slavery, our freedoms are in jeopardy. The following story illustrates the point.

Doing research on the Gulf oil spill for a project, I drove through Plaquemine Parish near New Orleans, LA, an area severely flooded by hurricane Katrina on August 28, 2005.

The effects of the oil spill were not visible, but the remnants of Katrina were everywhere. Following is a series of photographs taken in the drive through. One brave elderly man summarized the conditions in the area. He sadly explained the damage to the school, and the subsequent shutdown. He did not know how far students traveled to attend a different one. As he walked away, anger boiled up, that this human, in his old age, was living under these conditions.

The photographs are from March 2011. Why were these areas not rebuilt along with the rich coastal homes? The answer is Plaquemine Parish is poor, black and has little political power or influence. In the meantime, our country spent billions rebuilding Iraq and wasted billions on failed renewable-energy policies. Does anyone think this pattern is unique to New Orleans? The question is not why a black president failed to rebuild because George Bush also did little. The lesson is obvious. Power is color blind, and it is all about power.

This is not a conservative vs. liberal issue. It is an American tragedy perpetrated by both parties.

The sobering part of the trip was not being able to find anyone willing to talk about the oil spill and its effects. The Federal government appears to have shut down the free press. Most of the residents we talked to were afraid to discuss the situation because the government and BP had not settled with the litigants or silence was part of the agreement. Fear is the glue for enslavement.

Americans, through the Constitution and Bill of Rights, are free and equal people. The Constitution prevents the government from enslaving the people, either physically or mentally. Our government conceptually works for us, not vice-versa. The difference is profound. Serving at the will of the government translates to lost freedoms. We need to hold elected officials accountable for saying one thing and doing another.

This would be the one acceptable stereotype. Having the ability to walk among our fellow Americans, and find them tolerant and respectful of others. All are free, in mind, body, and spirit, to pursue happiness, prosperity, and self-fulfillment. All are equal, under God, the Stars and Stripes, and the law.

THE WASP IN THE WINDOW

August, 2013, Issue 2

Ushering in Church one Sunday, I observed a wasp fighting furiously to exit via a side window, separated from the open door by a six-inch support structure. The wasp repeatedly assaulted the pane, buzzing furiously in frustration. When the service ended and the congregation exited, a blast of air blew the insect backwards for several feet. The route to freedom now visible, the wasp escaped.

It was an enlightening observation creating a troubling analogy. Frequently in business while dealing with a constant flood of variables and preoccupation, the big picture becomes unfocused. The subtle shifts in behavior go unseen and the power of paradigm shifts propel us along into unexpected opportunities and minefields.

American business is still shaking off the recession, where belts were tightened, cash flow carefully watched, and investments judiciously controlled. The objective was survival and growth in a hostile environment. The future shows signs for optimism. A moment of reflection helps refocus on the reasons for being in business.

Last year, I had the good fortune to spend two days with more than four hundred entrepreneurs. The attendees were multi-racial from every conceivable background, and involved in business enterprises from primitive to super high technology. They formed in small groups and large, without regard for any differences, to discuss ideas and activities. Entrepreneurs with fifty years of experience helped novices, and high tech people worked with low-tech startups. Any idea was worth exploring, and collaboration was not some nebulous term, but the pathway to success.

Attendees went out of their way to introduce people with common interests. In participative meeting, commenting on materials each participant presented, all were brutally honest, positive, and helpful.

The two days were memorable, functioning in a world of total equality where everyone respected each other. In addition, there was a great deal of laughing, joking, and just enjoying each other's company without the social baggage.

These people were a microcosm of the day-to-day world, filled with distrust, racial tensions, liberal vs. conservative, oppositions between men and women - all these areas of conflict. How did this group of extraordinary people avoid this turmoil?

The answer is straightforward. They shared three common goals - build a successful business, make it grow, and invest in the future to grow ever larger. Pretensions are a luxury none could afford. Distractions were a waste of time. We talked about failures and lessons learned. It is implicit among entrepreneurs that success and failure are part of growth. Every entrepreneur knows how to take responsibility, and have the courage to get up and try again.

There are numerous reasons for working, from necessity to a dream, but most people work to make money to support families and priorities. The pursuit of passions is important, but without money, probably not obtainable. The concepts for personal solvency and actualization are the same as for business.

Some people in our society argue that money equates to corruption, but everyone needs it. There is an argument about how much individuals have (rich vs. poor), and redistribution, but these are discussions dealing with social and monetary policy. Money, in a business context, is neutral, neither good nor evil, while having the potential to be used for any purpose. Money is a tool to achieve dreams and increase the quality of life. Without money and solvency, there are no alms for the poor.

All business people need to share entrepreneurial goals, regardless of ownership or professional management.

- Make the business successful and profitable.
- Help the business grow by adding value.
- Build stockholder equity and reinvest it for productive purposes.

As individuals, when our contributions help achieve business goals, the intent is to profit, grow, save money and invest it where our interest lies.

Now is the time to step back and ask if the business strategies, practices, processes, and products align with these profoundly important objectives. Make sure customer service and quality are included in the thought processes. Review business values, including integrity, quality, safety, and environment.

Perform a comparative product analysis to establish marketplace potential and opportunity for product improvement and customer acceptance.

Review the ability of processes to meet the three objectives and identify potential improvements and programs to achieve them.

Evaluate how to initiate or improve collaboration programs with customers/suppliers, adding value to products, processes, and supply chains.

Employees are the most important business asset, and for all the rhetoric about involvement, the potential opportunities are largely untapped. Invite people into the business vision, and share the information they need to help you realize it.

The wasp escaped to an unknown future, but it was free to pursuit its goals. We need to free ourselves from artificial constraints and refocus on building our businesses.

Epilogue

Government and society in general are like the wasp. We observe unacceptable situations, but it takes time to process the data, analyze the causes, and realize the sometimes-horrible consequences. From all available material, President Obama is an excellent father and good husband. His election proved the possibilities for everyone in America. Without question, he had a mandate from the people. The problem is that his view of America is different, and his policies are proving to be contrary to who we are as people, and detrimental to our future as a country. He had the chance to be our national entrepreneur by applying the common principles of stated on Page 19.

Instead, President Obama took us on an unfamiliar path, and the destination is increasingly clear and frightening. That path and its potential result, will unfold through the subsequent Focused Fire Newsletters.

Sharpen the Focus on Business Fundamentals

September, 2013, Issue 4

The August Focused Fire Newsletter broadly addressed business fundamentals. To recap, all business people need to share entrepreneurial goals, regardless of ownership or professional management, and implement programs to achieve them.

- Make the business successful and profitable.
- Help the business grow by adding value.
- Build stockholder equity and reinvest it for productive purposes.

Periodically, leaders must step back and ask if the business strategies, practices, processes, and products align with these profoundly important objectives. Make sure customer service and quality are included in the thought processes.

Review business values, including integrity, quality, safety, and environment.

During recessions, management tightens control of every business facet, frequently severely limiting the inputs from associates. Conversely, when asking a businessperson for their competitive advantage, many will respond "our people." Test this in your organization. When was the last time the executive staff parked their computers and toured the shop floor, talking to people about their concerns and ideas for actually improving the business? Do associates have a valid mechanism for providing inputs? Are they in the information loop? Do HR policies make sense for your business model? Are one set of measurements used for performance and another for promotions or merit increases?

Employees are the most important business asset, and for all the rhetoric about involvement, the potential opportunities are largely untapped. Invite people into the business vision, and share the information they need to help you realize it.

Continuing to focus on human relationships, examine the quality of collaboration programs with customers and suppliers. These are profoundly critical opportunities, but normally under or poorly utilized. Evaluate how to initiate or improve programs adding value to people, relationships, products, processes, and supply chains.

Perform a comparative product analysis to establish marketplace potential and opportunity for product improvement and customer acceptance.

Review the ability of processes to meet the three objectives and identify potential improvements and programs to achieve them.

Contemporary corporate strategies are environmentally inclusive, targeting waste through process improvement programs and reduction of all types, including what/how much is recycled, repurposed, or discarded into the landfills. Your competitors may be actively implementing ISO 1401, and customers tracking your compliance.

Each point requires a total systems perspective, with details supporting the strategic conclusions. Rethink the issues, find supporting data, and convert the information into actionable form.

There are three operational areas, sharing strategic importance, where a more detailed assessment is beneficial. They are:

Enterprise planning - ERP/MRP, CRM
Process Improvement Programs – Lean, Lean Six Sigma, TOC, VMP
Supply Chain management and Supply Chain Collaboration

Epilogue

Federal budgets are based on the prior year's expenditures regardless of the department's real or residual value. For example, if an entity fails to spend its entire budget, cuts may occur. Additionally, expenditures aimed at influential constituency groups help politicians stay in office. For this reason, reducing cost is anathema, and the process improvement tools employed by private industry ignored. The resulting perpetual expansion of government consumes an ever-growing proportion of capital, decreasing the amount of money and resources available to fuel growth in the private sector.

Transformation in government is difficult but not impossible. Change takes leadership, conviction, courage, and incentive. These are rare traits, and probably in no greater supply with the Republican majority than with the Democratic administration recently relegated to minority status. That leaves us, the people, to facilitate change, but through engagement in the governance process, not by revolution. Apathy is the enemy of freedom, and a little dissent sends a clear message to our elected officials.

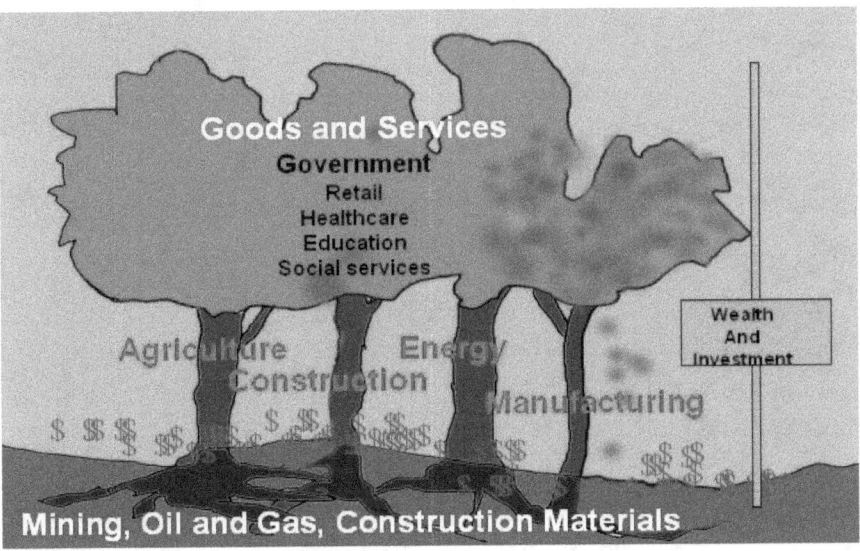

CHICKENS

November, 2013 Issue 5, Political Humor - Four photographs

Elected Democrats running from Obamacare

NSA Data Gatherings

IRS Profiling Conservatives

Benghazi

Fast and Furious

Unemployment Situation

Obama care

Leading from Behind

"The chickens will come home to roost"
Rev. Jeremiah Wright

House and Senate – Both Parties

Which side of the fence are you on?

Dumb question – mine.

Getting reelected and feathering their own nests are two subjects they agree on.

Why do the young have to pay for everything? Besides, where are the jobs?

Talk about chicken——!

My college loans cost me a fortune, and I need a job that pays more than minimum wage.

Is this called "generational theft"? It's too much, I want to get back into my shell and text someone - anyone.

Societies are judged by the world they leave to future generations!

POVERTY HURTS 24/7

December, 2013 Issue 6

Natalie and I, with a contingency of concerned citizens, recently toured the Marathon County, WI social service facilities, components of the United Way. The crowd moved ahead while I concentrated on capturing visual images. Photos taken, a chair in the hallway was welcome. Here was the view.

The lockers were in the hallway. Did they contain all the remaining resources for one person? Juxtaposed next to an image of storage units, possibly filled with the excess material possessions of many people, raises troubling questions about societal materialism, and wasted resources.

As these images clogged one part of consciousness, the experience of childhood and poverty slowly began to flood another part, and then they merged into one set of conclusions. The first merger point was recognition that poverty is real, not an abstract social discussion about redistribution.

26

Childhood

Our parents fought against their humble origins, but were unable to break the poverty continuum. There were eight family members, our parents and six children. Personally, Christmas was an annual reminder of the physical paucity and dark psychological deprivation that pounded at self-image. With few resources, the perception was that others had abundant affluence. Collectively among the siblings, the economic state, never discussed, is not a shared experience. None of us dared ask why, a forbidden question, partially out of fear and acceptance. In some children's minds, unasked questions are profound, as both symbols and reality.

Christmas began with a tree. A pagan symbol converted to Christian purpose, trees can be symbols of affluence. The rich had large "perfectly shaped" balsam firs, while each Christmas Eve afternoon, a farmer delivered a small, lowly cedar tree to our home. While rough in appearance, the cedar has a delightful, woodsy aroma, but I was ashamed of it. After decorating the tree and hanging stockings on the bench, we walked to Church, while other families drove cars.

My sisters and brothers impatiently spent the night, rising early to open presents. Reality was manifest in the type, number, and quality of gifts. Each child received one low priced gift and a stocking full of small items, mainly tangerines, candy, and underwear. By contrast, our friends appeared to receive unlimited amounts of cool stuff. On the day after Christmas, we discarded the tree.

Christmas dinner was a feast fit for royalty. Mom was an excellent cook, and the chicken or ham, potatoes, homemade cranberry sauce all exceeded gourmet standards. Mom sold her home baked bread for twenty cents a loaf, and unquestionably, these sales were the source for procuring our presents. Never, until much older, was it comprehended how much she gave up for what an ungrateful child perceived as so little.

Economic circumstances aside, Christmas was a joyful occasion. I have few memories of Dad but can picture Mom watching us. It is impossible to look into past moments and know what combinations of joy and pain she experienced. One can only hope she was content, doing everything in her power to bring Christmas to her family.

Christmas celebrations for the author ended one December 3. An ambulance came to our home, and a tearful mother informed her children, "Your father has died." I was sixteen, the youngest brother Glenn, only ten. For Mom, it meant widowhood and facing the grind of raising her family, while already in difficult circumstances, with virtually no income. One sister married shortly before Dad died, the other shortly after. I joined the Army upon reaching seventeen.

I angrily walked away from God, Christmas and for the most part, family, for the next six years, and my siblings started the migration from our hometown. The graves of our parent's, and one sister, Caryl, are all that remain.

Natalie and I were engaged fifty-two years ago, just prior to Christmas, a day she fully loves and celebrates for its religious meaning, the Birth of Christ, and the warmth of family and friends. She too, was born of humble circumstances, but her joy of life mostly carried her above the pain that I had experienced. Two of her characteristics bridge the differences in our perceptions, her extraordinary faith foundation, and rejection of materialism.

For our first Christmas as a married couple, I cut a perfectly shaped little tree. We proudly decorated and admired its beauty. Upon returning from Christmas with her family, the needles had fallen off. The tree was not a Balsam, but a lowly little Tamarac, which sheds its needles each year much as oak or maple. She calls it our "Charlie Brown Christmas tree" and we laugh when thinking about it.

Our children returned the great joys of Christmas to my heart. We had trees, presents, great food, love, and faith in the birth of Christ and its celebration. Presents are physical manifestations of love, more important to some, less so to others, but it was pure joy watching the kids tear open the packages, laughing and playing.

For our family, infinitudes of "Thank you, God" are inadequate.

Conclusions

The great recession and sluggish recovery have increased poverty throughout society, and many people suffer profoundly from its effects. Poverty hurts 24/7, and it strikes hardest at the young members of society.

Material possessions, as envisioned by a child, are confused between needs and want. Mired in the relentless state of deprivation, it may be difficult to discern the difference. The curse of poverty is not just a shortage of goods and services, but also the destruction of self-image.

Adults must never underestimate the peer effect on children. Gifts of food, clothing, and objects to match those of peers are important to build positive self-images. How can people help themselves without believing a different reality is possible and they own the opportunity?

In addition, the value of resources is quality of utilization, not quantity. For families, the gifts under the tree are important. As children, there was never a food shortage for Christmas, for either Nat or myself, but some items remained scare at times. Our Mom's frugal habits, chicken coops, and cooking ability kept hunger away. Today, the resource mix has changed. In many cases, food stamps are available. While children may not be starving in the streets, the insidious effects of malnutrition are pervasive with lifetime effects.

On Christmas day, and throughout the year, the greatest expression of our love is making sure there are resources available for those in need. Nothing on Christmas replaces the joys of a child opening what may be a life-changing gift. Happiness is parents somehow able to bring Christmas peace to their families with needed food, clothing, shelter, a Christmas tree, and gifts to put under it.

Poverty may hurt 24/7, but on Christmas day, we collectively have the power to relieve the pain for every person, every family in need. Once the festivities are over, the needs will remain, and society (we the people) must wage a perpetual war against its insidious effects.

Give generously to the local charities focusing contributions very precisely to the point of need. For the Wausau, WI area, these include your local churches and:

- United Way of Marathon County
- The Women's Community
- Wausau Community Warming Center
- Salvation Army
- Catholic Charities
- St Vincent DePaul

Merry Christmas and Happy New Year,

Epilogue

The first inclination was to eliminate this newsletter from the book. On reflection, the conditions described are partially the result of the economic decline, redistribution, and downsizing of America.

There are concerned persons, many retired, working diligently to fill the voids created by the lack of fiscal, monetary and economic policies by the governing officials. In the meantime, every election cycle, candidates and political parties spend billions of dollars shaping the vote. Elections rise and fall on emotional issues while children go to bed hungry, and with young people trapped in the spiral of poverty, literally without hope or opportunity.

Why are we concerned about abstractions when the problems are not somewhere else, but right next to us? Why do we elect people to govern, and then fight among ourselves when they fail to do the job? Where are our national priorities? Has America lost its moral foundation? Why are we not building an opportunity society where everyone has a chance to reach his or her potential? Have we lost the courage of conviction? If so, why are we afraid, and of what? Have fear, pacifism, and political correctness, enslaved us? If the answer is yes, it is time to play taps over what was once the greatest, and the freest country in the world.

Although written at two points in time, the next newsletter, "Why," is a continuation of this thought and questioning.

WHY?

January, 2014 Issue 7

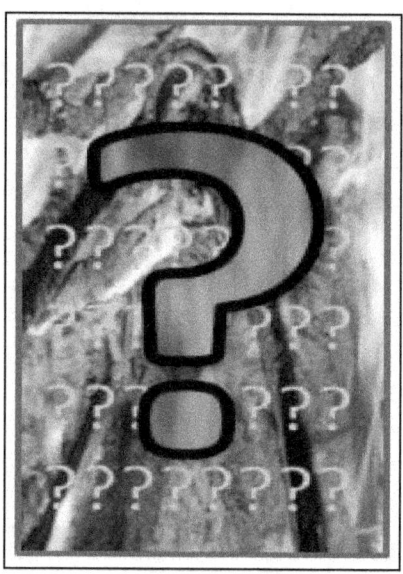

While on a research trip to the Gulf of Mexico, I had a strange dream that continues to jolt my consciousness, not hauntingly but as a subtle reminder.

As the dream unfolded, I am riding an ATV on a strange, oil slick, dark road with mud-like, but glassy texture. All structure and life were totally absent until I approached two racially mixed boys, sitting on this strange substance, dressed in patched but spotlessly clean clothes. The oldest, about four, was repairing a nondescript device while the smaller boy, quiet throughout the encounter, played with a broken toy truck.

I asked the older boy, "Where is everyone?"

He looked up with the sweetest face, his eyes clear and tearless, answering almost in a whisper, "Gone, they are all gone. There's just me and my brother."

"Where did they go?"

"I don't know."

He returned his attention to the device, than looking up, the serene, inquisitive look still etched in his young face, asked, "Why"?

Desperately searching for an answer, I quietly explained, "Well, hurricane Katina may have washed everything away."

"No, not that", he replied quietly.

I woke up, struggling for answers, aware the child's question was more profound and inclusive than the response. Unfolding like a sequel, the dream reemerged and focused on the children. Before I could speak, the boy, with face calm and beatific, asked again with infinite patience,

"Why?"

The dream, strange and confused, had two simultaneous endings. First, it faded, and then I simply rode away. The latter ending raised a question - if there was no one to care for them, why had I not taken the boys to safety. Eventually the answer materialized. Imagined into existence, they are home, locked solidly into my heart and conscience, catalysts for inquiry and antidotes for apathy.

As systems analysts, the words, what, why, when, where, and how, are essential fact-finding and problem solving questions. Our mobile technological society is obsessed with "what," searching Google and instantly equating the finding as facts.

The Five Why's is an improvement concept, introduced by Taiichi Ohno, the master behind the Toyota Production system. The Five Whys are a tool for systematic problem identification and resolution, and inclusive in Lean, Lean Six/Sigma, and Value Management Programs (VMP).

Wikipedia has done a great job of defining the concept.

> The 5 Whys is an iterative question-asking technique used to explore the cause-and-effect relationships underlying a particular problem. The primary goal of the technique is to determine the root cause of a defect or problem. (The "5" in the name derives from an empirical observation on the number of iterations typically required to resolve the problem.) http://en.wikipedia.org/wiki/5_Whys - cite_note-1

Foundational to curiosity, the significant question is to ask why. While obscured, there is always a cause and effect. Questions range from the macro to the minuscule. The answer to a question, such as "why do some individuals find it easy to forfeit their freedoms?" is both complicated and controversial. Some people have reservations about posing contentious questions, while others ask why, seeking clarity, facts, and truth. Without knowledge of the causes for an action/inaction, the effects lack clarity and rationality. Refusing to ask relevant questions measures our fear, not intellectual relevancy, and perpetuates the situation.

Given the challenge from the little boy, what remains is the application of the tools and defining solutions. First, we will state an unequivocal fact and provide the data. The United States is by far the richest, most successful county in the world. We passionately want to perpetuate this success for our children - all of the children.

The following chart shows the richest countries in the world, starting with the USA, greater than 16 trillion dollars, nearly twice that of China. This chart puts the narrative into perspective.

Country	2012 GDP
United States	16,244,600,000,000
China	8,227,102,629,831
Japan	5,959,718,262,199
Germany	3,428,130,624,839
France	2,612,878,387,760
United Kingdom	2,471,783,570,300
Brazil	2,252,664,120,777
Russian Federation	2,014,774,938,342
Italy	2,014,669,579,720
India	1,841,709,755,679
Canada	1,821,424,139,311

http://data.worldbank.org/indicator/NY.GDP.MKTP.CD

Following is a partial list of whys, and each reader will expand it with his or her own questions.

Given the United States is the richest country, why should any citizen be hungry or without healthcare?

Given the vast resources and state of our nation, why do we not have a collective mission statement?

Why continue to ignore waste in government and why not hold elected officials accountable?

Why are we the people fighting with each other instead of against non-responsive, corrupted government officials?

Americans value honesty and justice, so why not hold our government accountable for its deception and lies? Why does it matter unless we are complicit through apathy or political affiliation?

Why has fear stilled our voices, and sapped the courage to speak for our children?

Why, given that Americans spend more for education than any other country, do we rank 17th among the industrialized nations. Only 75% of our students graduate from high school. Source: http://thelearningcurve.pearson.com/the-report/towards-an-index-of-education-outputs

Why, given the amount of money spent on public education, do students at Catholic schools, receiving zero governmental funding, score consistently 10-20 points higher? Source: The Nations Report Card, Department of Education

Why do children go to school hungry? Source: http://feedingamerica.org/.

Why must Title 1 teachers beg for school supplies from their family members? Source: www.wkrn.com/story/21858334/supplieshttp://www.huffingtonpost.com/2012/08/23/survey-many-teachers-repo_n_1822777.html

Given that pollution is global, why do Americans look the other way as China builds coal power plants, and we dismantle coal production in the United States? Why are their cheap products more important than our environmental values?

Why, given the resources available, do disaster areas such as Plaquemine Parish and New Jersey still need rebuilding funds?

The little boys in my dream are an incarnation of our children and grandchildren, who always ask why. They are a manifestation of our responsibility to future generations. It must be a colorblind future with opportunities for all. Dr. Corina Norrbom, a guest presenter on CompetitiveAmerica.us, posted a paper titled "Is It Good for the Children?" Her presentation neatly summarizes society's obligation to future generations.

Based on Dr. Norrbom's criteria, some evaluative questions are required, about how well we are achieving this objective.

Why have we burdened future generations with an ultra expensive healthcare system?

Why are we allowing our government to erode the very rights our children deserve?

Why perpetuate an education system teaching our students what, instead of how to think?

Why does our education system leave graduates thousands of dollars in debt?

Why not re-engineer and address the education system, matching degrees to employer's requirements with an integrated college and technical school system?

Why are future generations burdened with a national debt (18 trillion dollars, greater than one year of national GDP) requiring them to pay higher interest and taxes for a lifetime?

Why have we not fixed the social security system, making it available for future generations, instead of subsidizing seniors on the backs of the young?

Why have we created a business environment where job development is discouraged through governmental regulations, resulting in high unemployment among the young?

Why are we not creating a society where children can vision big, and then work to make those passions a reality?

Why have we created a society where, for the first time in American history, the future prospects for our children and grandchildren are less than prior generations?

The dream children permeated my conscience, dramatically escalating the challenge to take action. Society is failing our children, facing futures with reduced opportunities, a remarkable broken continuum. Ask if you are responsible for their future, because if not, their fate is sealed. If yes, take the time to honestly answer these questions, and ask "why" five times to each answer to find the root cause.

The American people will differ on questions and answers (solutions), and reflect the disagreement with our divided government. While all are required to fix the problems, there must first be an honest, civil dialogue. Currently, many carefully avoid controversial issues, even among family members. Perhaps all need more courage to ask important questions, hopefully in a non-confrontational way. Nothing positive will result until we bury the conflict between liberals, conservatives, et al, confronting common issues as one people.

Once defined, ask what actions will fix the problems, than take positive steps to implement solutions. If we care enough, then positive changes will occur, enabling future generations to blossom like flowers on the new tree of opportunity, entrepreneurialism, and prosperity.

Epilogue

The "WHY" newsletter is the genesis to the book, and precipitated the investigation backing up every Focused Fire Newsletter.

Our readers will disagree on cause and effect, options and solutions. These debates are welcome because honest inquiry and dialogue lead to enlightenment and solutions.

DEFINING QUALITY

February, 2014 Issue 8

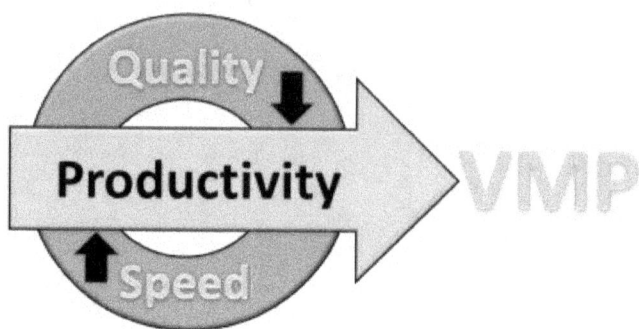

Value Management Program

Quality has long been a planned topic for the Focused Fire Newsletter. Competitive America is a staunch ally of American manufacturing, and quality is involved in all of our books and training materials. Defining quality, from a functional and pragmatic viewpoint, is not simple. For that reason, we waited for the appropriate examples.

Philip B. Crosby, author of "Quality is Free," defines quality as conformance to requirements (not as goodness).

In practice, the definition and context changes with viewpoint. For example, manufacturing may define it as conformance to design and specifications, while a customer measures it by how well it meets expectations and needs. Health care measures quality in terms of patient outcomes. A different measurement is value perception as a product and its associated usefulness. Product is available at all levels of quality and price, consistent with its value and affordability to the customer.

Quality is also situational, sometimes as a tradeoff to value. For example, a bottle of water costs less than one dollar in normal circumstances, and an ounce of gold, greater than $1200.

If dying of thirst in the desert, a sane person would quickly choose (value) the water over the gold.

From a purely practical perspective, most judge quality by how well the product performs or how positive the experience is with the seller or service provider.

For the last ten years, with the help of two brothers-in-law, our MTD snow blower has done a great job of removing the snow from our central Wisconsin driveway, along with the mess created by the snowplow. We welded on a new bottom, and when the control cables continued to break, installed homemade, heavier gauge cables solved the problem. The root problem, however, was the slow disintegration of the machine, and replacing it the only logical decision.

41

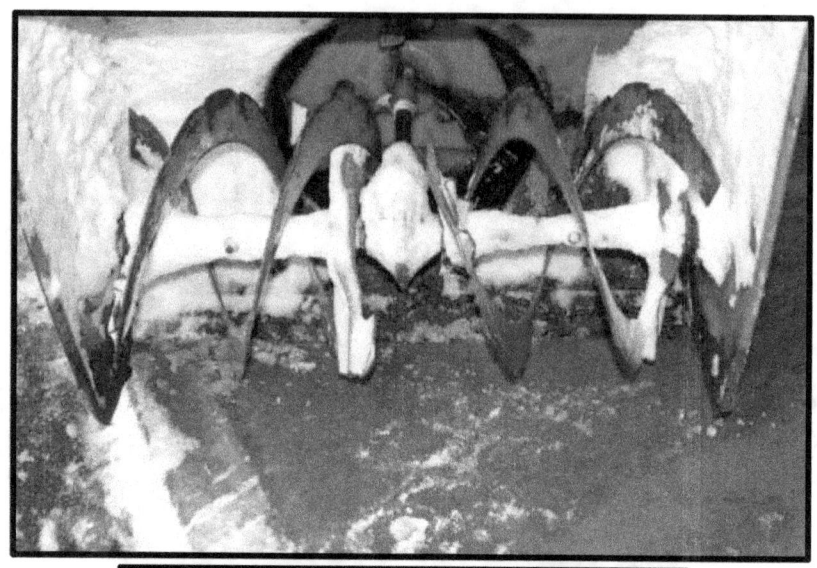

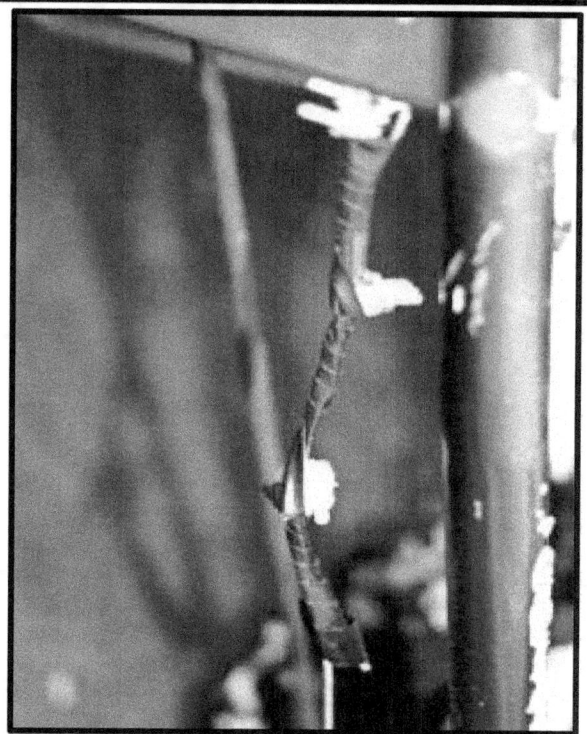

I preselected a snow blower, after an extensive internet search, based on two points of bias. First, Affinity Systems has a long association with the New North, an exciting and vibrant economic consortium involving 18 counties in northeastern Wisconsin, and second, a quality Wisconsin manufacturer located in the New North makes the product.

An ad published in the daily newspaper featured the preselected unit and on October 17, I looked at one, rated to handle up to 16" of snow, approximately the same as the MTD. It had several cool attributes the MTD lacks, lights and a feature called Auto-Turn, intended to "optimize maneuverability." Lacking availability, including the floor model, but preferring to buy from local sources, and with plenty of time for delivery, I purchased a unit. After a follow-up telephone call, the dealer delivered on November 13, 2013.

The new machine cleared several fluffy snowfalls in November and December, but proved unable to track in a straight line, requiring extreme force to "dig" into the piles left by the snowplow. When the job was finished, a buildup of snow residue remained next to the road, an unacceptable result. Likewise, there was too much leftover on the entire driveway, a condition potentially resolved by adjusting the shoes. The new machine was benched, and the MTD promptly removed the snow buildup down to the pavement.

With Christmas nearing and the family home for the holidays, the new machine remained parked, while the MTD kept the driveway clear for our guests.

Normalcy returned, and on January 4, 2014, I stopped by the dealer to explain the situation. The sales person said they would fix the problems and called the service department, located in a different building. After a long wait, the service man stated there would be charges for pickup and delivery. After I complained it was a new unit, he relented and set up a pickup for the following Monday. It was extremely cold on that day, with no pick up, and that is understandable, and no call, which is poor customer feedback. Another call on Thursday resulted in a pickup on Friday, January 10.

The first major snowstorm blanketed the area overnight on January 14.

The newspaper headline was **"STORM LEAVES CHAOS"**

The MTD snow blower made short work of the project, removing the nine inches of snow and residual from the snowplow.

It no longer has a classy appearance, but with the chips down, the MTD made short work of the project, without lights or auto-turn, and that is quality performance. I was grateful for its availability, but wondered how the new machine would have operated.

Several days later, it snowed approximately four inches, a perfect test for the new machine, but while beautiful and sophisticated, it was in the shop, and that equals zero quality and performance by default. After one week, waiting for communication regarding its availability, I called one of the owners at the dealership and the machine arrived the next day.

Used frequently since its return January 21, the machine suffers from the same problems identified earlier, and three of the small plastic components broke when it was cold. These are fixable with the application of experimentation and innovation, but one of the major reasons for the purchase was eliminating excessive maintenance.

I believe manufacturing meticulously complied with every quality specification. The problems have two origins. The Auto-Turn feature is an engineering innovation to make work easier, but the technology introduced imprecision. The plastic pieces and other quality issues probably result from process improvement projects reducing quality instead of increasing value. If not, shame on design engineering.

The new machine will eventually replace the MTD but regardless of its potential, it passed the rule of "conformance to requirements," but failed the critical tests of quality performance and customer satisfaction. The new machine will probably always be subpar to the MTD, but bought and paid for, it must reside in that awful quality bracket labeled "good enough."

There are lessons learned and relearned. I need to re-examine the bias towards Wisconsin manufacturers and practice better due diligence. While everyone likes more bells and whistles, it may not translate into better performance. Carefully select quality local retailers who have provided positive customer experiences to friends and relatives.

Our old Toro lawn tractor is in a parallel situation. Like the MTD, it gets the job done, but is aging and requires increasing amounts of maintenance. When it gets warm in Wisconsin, I will disassemble and repair it if possible, and if not, make an evidenced based decision on both a manufacturer and retailer to replace it. The purchase will involve a local supplier, keeping the money circulating in our economy, and providing jobs and services. The product label will be "made in America," and it must exceed the capabilities of the old.

The decision to exclude the names of the dealer and producer reflect the intent to define quality, not air grievances. There is insufficient data for a broad performance evaluation, given a population of one, but the incident itself is personally significant, and a great example for this paper on quality.

In the final analysis, quality is in the eyes of the beholder, in terms of esthetics, performance, service, and value. We expect conformance to specifications. Consumers will use their pocket books to cast the final vote on product and service quality.

Epilogue - 9-20-2014

The new snow thrower is gone, given to a person in a state with considerably less snow than Wisconsin. The very things I disliked about the machine are advantages in the different environment. As for the old Toro lawn tractor, repaired, it works great.

Our society once again accepts inferior quality in products, personal relationships, and government. Our landfills overflow with junk, much of it from offshore suppliers. Quality products last longer, are more reliable, and recyclable. An opportunity society embraces a dedicated passion for quality, performance, resource conservation, entrepreneurship, and excellence, as tools for rebuilding America.

Do the Means Justify the End?

March, 2014 Issue 9

Last month's Focused Fire Newsletter pursued the definition of quality, and found the subject more complicated than it would outwardly appear. In comparison, defining what the word truth means is even more complicated, but relates absolutely to the essence of our personal relationships, social fabric, and our position in a competitive world.

Upon discovery, lying and/or deceiving potentially results in angry consequences, with reaction often proportionately more severe than the lie itself. The greatest casualty is a loss of trust and respect. There will be accountability in some form, perhaps severe. The best resolution is taking responsibility, admission, and accountability. Regaining trust requires investment in the relationship, and honest actions, not words. This presumes others are considered to be worthy of an apology, and continuing relationship.

Match this private reaction to the public tolerance of near pathological lying by our elected officials on both sides, even after the lie is irrefutable. President Lyndon Johnson lied about sending troops to Vietnam. President Nixon lied about the Watergate break-in and later resigned. The electorate held President George H. Bush accountable for raising taxes after he promised, "Read my lips: no new taxes." President Clinton lied when he said, "I did not have sex with that woman," and was impeached, but not convicted.

Accusations often have an impact similar to exposure. For example, many think that President George W. Bush lied about weapons of mass destruction in Iraq. History must sort out the facts, and if true, the lie was certainly significant.

Few lies reach the magnitude or frequency of President Obama's "If you like your health care plan, you can keep your health care plan, period." It was a deception constructed to sell the Affordable Care Act, a massive governmental takeover of health care, to legislators and the public. Future generations will judge the value gained/lost from reengineering one-sixth of the American economy through subterfuge.

The polls show a substantial drop in President Obama's trustworthiness, yet he continues to compound the problem. In an interview with Bill O'Reilly on FOX news, he stated there is "not a smidgen of corruption," on the part of the IRS, even as evidence to the contrary continues to build.

Obviously, there is something missing in all of this besides the truth.

In May 2001, former CBS News anchor Dan Rather stated, when asked about President Clintons' honesty, "Well, because I think he is. I think at core he's an honest person. I know that you have a different view. I know that you consider it sort of astonishing anybody would say so, but I think you can be an honest person and lie about any number of things."

In a CNN interview, Ed Uravic, author of "Lying Cheating Scum" said "Every president has not only lied at some time, but needs to lie to be effective,"

The core perspective is how we perceive truth and consequences.

Most of us live by deontological ethics, or judge the truth by the act/deed itself. The opposite viewpoint is consequentialism, where the end consequence determines the merits/truth of the deed/action. Stated a different way, consequentialism translates to "the end justifies the means."

One example of the latter paradigm is the Affordable Health Care Act (ACA).

In his sales pitch for the ACA, President Obama repeated a litany of promises.

> "If you like your health care you can keep your health care
> If you like your doctor, you can keep your doctor
> Obamacare won't add 'one dime to our deficits'
> Premiums will fall by as much as $2,500 per family."

The Affordable Care Act, passed in 2010, is the signature legislation of the Obama administration, passed entirely along party lines using deceit, lies, and strong-arm tactics. To get the last needed vote from Sen. Bart Stupak and the Pro-life Senatorial vote, President Obama signed an Executive Order barring federal funding of abortion through the Affordable Care Act.

Several years later Mr. Stupak said,

> "I am perplexed and disappointed that, having negotiated the Executive Order with the President, not only does that HHS mandate violate the Executive Order but it also violates statutory law . . . . I think it is illegal."

(Note: The ACA allows abortions, and the Executive order stands in direct contradiction).

Every one of the above promises proved to be falsehoods, some to sell the program, and others as deceit to keep 2012 voters from finding out the negative ramifications of the legislation. The troubling question is

50

whether, in his mind, they are lies or just necessary deceit to achieve his vision.

Sold under the premises of "the means justifies the end" philosophy, the net result of the ACA will be unknown until well after President Obama is out of office. It raises a greater question; do the American people call this a truthful process deserving a reward?

Yet, President Obama did not act alone, and the authors of the bill were a combination of business and political people. Every Democratic Senator and Representative voted for the Bill without reading it, an astonishing display of arrogance and irresponsibility to the people empowering them. Obviously, by default or intent, they practiced the philosophy of "any means justifies the end," hoping the end result would be positive, and constituents reward them with additional terms in office. In my opinion, voters need to oust politicians violating the public's trust.

The press upon which the public once relied for honest reporting apparently abdicated responsibility in reporting the ACA, either buying the "any means" argument, or were so deeply bias the truth was invisible. Frequently, dishonesty in the press is omission, sitting on information needed by the public to make evidence-based decisions. While researching our book Crunch Time for Health Care, and the later version Productivity Prescriptions for Health Care, Jon Bingol and I had little difficulty finding and anticipating the major flaws in the ACA, and extrapolating the considerable consequences. Largely ignored, the issues still must approach the crisis stage before coverage by the mainstream press. In defense of the press, no one wants to listen to the problems, including family and friends. Sadly, the worst features of the law have received little attention. In my personal bias, the modern press was absorbed into, and then abdicated to the political process, failing its role to keep the public honestly informed. In our rewrite, "Productivity Prescriptions for Health Care," scheduled for publication in April, Jon and I focus on actions that health care must take to brunt the effects of the ACA.

Voters may be blind to the deceptions because they trusted Obama to seize the opportunity and achieve positive change. That luster has not entirely rubbed off. Others looked past the dishonesties of the politician to the man, apparently an honest husband and good father. By their votes, all accepted the "any means to an end" argument. The end game for this administration remains unclear, and the rules constantly change, by obvious intent and deception. The key analogy is an iceberg, where the tip represents known lies, but hidden beneath the waves floats a mass of negative consequences.

The "any means justifies the end" philosophy breaks down quickly at the personal level. Telling one's spouse "I'm having an affair for the good of the marriage" will fly for one nanosecond. Why then, do we allow our elected officials to lie without accountability? Often failing to perform due diligence, the result is what we deserve.

Citizens need to fight for a truthful, honest, and accountable government. When officials establish their own agenda and use deception to achieve it, they eventually lose the confidence of the people and become irrelevant. Without a democratic process, we are enslaved and our freedoms lost. Meanwhile, the country will drift without leadership, from one crisis to another, exerting little influence over world events.

America needs a rebirth of truth and honesty, restoring our integrity and providing a common purpose, to build a competitive America.

Epilogue

Sometimes other people's words make a better point for us. After discussions on "for the greater good" and "trust," the following is a powerful reinforcement of our position.

> "According to video posted Friday (November 7, 2014) by American Commitment, a conservative group, Massachusetts Institute of Technology professor Jonathan Gruber delivered

remarks in October 2013 during which he explained the "tortured way" Obamacare was written that enabled its passage.

"This bill was written in a tortured way to make sure CBO did not score the mandate as taxes," detailed Gruber. "If [Congressional Budget Office] scored the mandate as taxes, the bill dies. Okay, so it's written to do that. In terms of risk-rated subsidies, if you had a law which said that healthy people are going to pay in — you made explicit that healthy people pay in and sick people get money — it would not have passed."

"Lack of transparency is a huge political advantage," he continued. "And basically, call it the stupidity of the American voter, or whatever, but basically that was really, really critical to getting the thing to pass. And it's the second-best argument."

http://redalertpolitics.com/2014/11/10/obamacare-architect-jonathan-gruber-law-passed-thanks-lack-transparency/#ZHpDjlUrwp8Jb8Fx.99

There were at least four videos of Jonathan Gruber, one of the primary architects of the Affordable Care Art, calling the citizens of America "stupid." He was deeply involved in writing the Massachusetts health care program implemented by then Governor Romney. The Obama administration, capitalizing on the expertise gained on that program hired Mr. Gruber to help develop the ACA.

His name will be in the headlines as the Supreme Court debates the issues of subsides for the states. In summary, the administration argues the subsidies apply to all the states, whether in the exchange or not.

"What's important to remember politically about this is if you're a state and you don't set up an exchange, that means your citizens don't get their tax credits—but your citizens still pay the taxes that support this bill. So you're essentially saying [to] your citizens you're going to pay all the taxes to help all the other states in the country. I hope that that's a blatant enough

political reality that states will get their act together and realize there are billions of dollars at stake here in setting up these exchanges. But, you know, once again the politics can get ugly around this.
http://reason.com/blog/2014/07/24/watch-obamacare-architect-jonathan-gruber

The press was aware of, but chose not to report on the video.

It will be hard to find a better example of the concept of the "means justifies the end," and how it can translate into "my way or the highway," than the Affordable Health Care Act. How can a victimized constituency trust a government that defrauds them, or a press complicit with the fraud? In a very predictable response, the White House, elected officials and the press are in full recovery mode, all throwing Jonathan Gruber under the bus.

The controversy and associated costs of the ACA will worsen. President Obama shifted the truly expensive and contentious implementation items until he is out of office. For details see: http://www.nejm.org/doi/full/10.1056/NEJMp1403294

When examining the health care issue with any degree of objectivity, there are unpleasant truths. Prior to the passage of the ACA, health care costs were spiraling out of control. Nearly 50 million Americans lacked adequate access to health care.

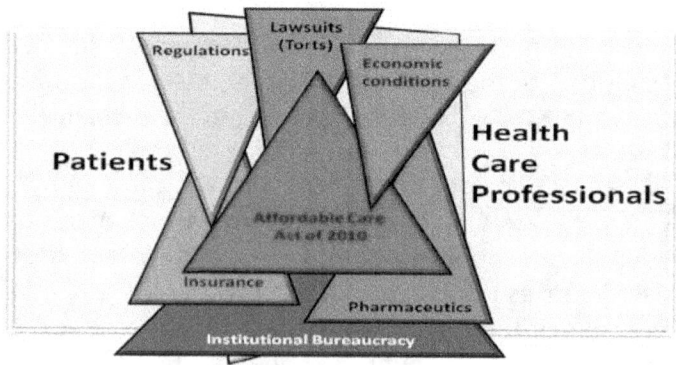

The above chart, from <u>Productivity Prescriptions for Health Care</u>, shows wedges driven between the patient and health care provider. Each wedge adds cost and inefficiency to the process. The Affordable Care Act layered additional bureaucracy over the top of an already costly bureaucracy. A more effective approach would involve examining each of these wedges and shrinking each one down to a controllable size.

In the richest country on earth, every citizen should have access to affordable and comprehensive health care. Unless the system is converted back into a market-based system, and the wedges reduced, universal coverage is not achievable.

In a perverse way, Mr. Gruber's honesty was refreshing. He revealed the ACA as a hoax. It will not achieve the goal of providing affordable health care to every American citizen in spite of how much of our money the government spends.

Further exploring the topic of "the means justifying the end," one need only read Saul Alinsky's Rules for Radicals to understand President Obama's attitude on the subject.

> "The man of action views the issue of means and ends in pragmatic and strategic terms. He has no other problem; he thinks only of his actual resources and the possibilities of various choices of action. He asks of ends only whether they are achievable and worth the cost; of means, only whether they will work. To say that corrupt means corrupt the ends is to believe in the immaculate conception of ends and principles."

President Obama is a disciple of Alinsky. He taught workshops at the Developing Communities Project using his method. Obama worked with ACORN, another Alinsky creation. He obviously believes the means justify the end, and he wants to determine both the means and the end.

How can a society trust a leader who operates with different ethics, and those ethics are in conflict with national values? This may be acceptable for a dictator, but not the president of a democracy.

Happy Mother's Day

May, 2014 Issue 11

May is for Mother's Day, but it provides an opportunity for all men to honor the women in their lives. This newsletter is to tell all the women in my life they are loved, and thank you for enriching my life.

Throughout history, in many places and forms, women were/are treated as second-class citizens. The justification is that women were subordinate to men. In some situations, family fortunes go to sons, ignoring daughters.

Fortunately, there is a generational progression of women, each building on the strengths of the previous. Unfortunately, progress is not worldwide. I love and am very proud of my brothers, son, and sons-in-laws, grandsons, and grand-son-in-law but this newsletter pays tribute to the women in my life.

In our home as a child, life moved at the direction of a steely four foot nine inch tall woman, intolerant of inequality. Mom treated everyone the same and drilled that core message into her children. Widowed and trapped in a poverty situation, she succeeded in obtaining moderate wealth through hard work and frugal living. One of my sisters is now a great-grand mother, and the other joined Mom, Dad, and my youngest brother in God's hands.

My mother-in-law was a strong woman, managing a farm while raising twelve children as her husband worked in Milwaukee, returning home on weekends.

Both women experienced the Great Depression, profoundly affecting values and actions. It is amazing they could surmount tremendous adversities. Both were exceptionally intelligent women who never had an opportunity for higher education. The world is poorer for their passing, but by most measurements, they lived fulfilled lives.

My wife is an advocate for life, and despises abortion but not the girls desperately seeking them as a last resort. This is not anti-feminism, it is pro-life, and the terms need not conflict. She sees and treats people as equal. One of her core life goals was providing superior education for our four children, who graduated from a college prep private school system, draining the pocketbook. With three students in college, she took a menial job without complaint, spending virtually every cent on education. Work was never about her, and like mothers throughout history, investment for the future equates to investment in her children. She centers my life.

Our three daughters worked while attending, then graduating from college, one obtaining a Master's degree. Our daughter-in-law continues to fight for her dreams. All are rightly intolerant of discrimination, and have elevated life to a greater level. We are very proud of them.

Our granddaughters are bright, vibrant, and intelligent. The oldest has finished her undergraduate degree and need only finish her thesis to get a Masters from Columbia University. The second recently graduated from college and she is participating in the workplace. Our youngest is active in sports, music and does well in school. Without a doubt, they will elevate life yet another notch.

They have work to do. Other women in the world suffer horribly. I have two new heroes. The first is Malala Yousafzai, shot as a ninth-grader by the Pakistani Taliban for advocating girl's rights. Recovered, she is now running a worldwide campaign for education. Ayaan Hirsi Ali, who suffered growing up in Somalia, is second. The discrimination followed her to America. Brandeis University denied her an honorary degree for speaking the truth about growing up in a specific Muslim culture that disrespects and mutilates women.

Pray for the 276 Nigerian schoolgirls recently kidnapped by the terrorist group Boko Haram and sold as wives or shared among the soldiers. Underreported in the media for three weeks, civilized people everywhere should be outraged. It is a constant and brutal reminder of the thin line between barbarism and civilized behavior, and how little people care when it is "invisible." Equality and love cannot stop at our front door.

Epilogue

Many women throughout the world are in a worsening situation. The Nigerian students remain under the custody of their captors, who rampage the countryside, abducting additional girls. On January 3, the Boko Haram over-run the city of Baga, slaughtering an unknown number of the populace.

The Islamic State, ISIS, has taken atrocities against women to new levels of horror. ISIS has abducted and raped thousands of women, including little children, young, married, and elderly, and wantonly slaughtered unknown numbers of women, children, and men. Of those raped, there were more than 3,000 Yazidi. Many killed themselves after members of ISIS had satisfied their sadistic objectives.

Ayaan Hirsi Ali continues to meet resistance for speaking out against the abuse of women.

We live in a country where political parties argue about women's rights, and women vote for politicians that make birth control cheap. We fight for the right to abort unwanted babies, while the women in the Muslim world cringe in horror while terrible people rape and kill them, and the world does little about it. It is the same story - that is, as long as it is not in our back yard.

ISIS does not respect America, who lacked the moral courage to help these desperate people until the political outrage forced some token action. In fact, our early withdrawal from Iraq without a status of force's agreement set the stage for ISIS. We speak of respect for women, but like so many issues, America has become a paper tiger that no one respects, full of hot air, and reluctant to take action. Sadly, our country is now a reflection of our leadership.

That is a travesty.

TRUST

June, 2014 Issue 12

"You may fool all the people some of the time; you can even fool some of the people all the time; but you can't fool all of the people all of the time." Abraham Lincoln

Trust is the glue for civilized interaction and essential for sustaining all relationships, whether personal, business, or political. While an intangible, trust is one of the most powerful words in our vocabulary.

In a society, at work, at home or as part of our religion, there are shared values, including ethics, morals, and implied responsibilities for others. Obviously, religions and populations throughout the world have different value systems. In many cases, although flawed logic, people interpret shared values as being for the greater good, and violation of standards results in distrust and soiled reputations. In some countries, the consequences are extremely severe.

Reputation is one measure of trust. If people are truthful, honest, and fair in their dealing, and have personal integrity, most enjoy favorable reputations even when others disagree with their politics or perspectives. People with good reputations find it easier to get things done and participate in commercial activities. The reason, people trust them to do the job and do it right. Logically, everyone fails at some point, and trust implies accountability and taking responsibility, thereby starting the process of rebuilding trust. Given a lack of contrition for failure in relationships, additional distrust replaces what might otherwise start a healing process.

Following are key elements of trust that intertwine and support each other. These are honesty, quality, and integrity, being there for each other and forgiveness when possible or requested. We are all measured on how well we walk the talk, and keep promises and commitments.

Not telling the truth, either by out-right lying or through deception, has consequences. Friedrich Nietzsche summed it up neatly, "I'm not upset that you lied to me, I'm upset that from now on I can't believe you."

Given that trust is the fabric of our society, how do American institutions measure up?

Financial Institutions

CHICAGO (February 7, 2014) Americans are fed up with the excessive compensation and lack of integrity of top corporate managers, according to the latest data from the Chicago Booth/Kellogg School Financial Trust Index. The overall index's collective measure of trust held steady at 24 percent. Chase Financial institutions

Government

Following are the results of the Harvard University's Institute of Politics, trust levels from Millennials.

	2010	2014	Delta
Federal Gov	29%	20%	<09>
President	44%	32%	<12>
Congress	25%	14%	<11>
Supreme Court	45%	36%	<09>
Total	143	102	<41>
Average	35.75	25.5	<10.5>
Total average change			<28.7> % total
US Military	53%	47%	<06>
United Nations	40%	34%	<06>
Wall Street	11%	12%	01
The Media	17%	11%	<06>
NSA		24%	

This slice of our population represents our future. The numbers among other demographics vary, but these serve our purpose. The confidence, or trust, in our three governmental bodies has dropped by 28.7% in the last four years, trending downwards each year. Business fares no better, with the same approximate percentage approval as overall government. The most distressing number is that Millennials have greater trust in the United Nations than in America.

Given this data, what conclusions are drawn?

It is a given that much of the mistrust is caused by lies that become increasingly obvious to everyone. These include Benghazi, use of the IRS and other governmental agencies for political good, fast and furious, the Veterans Administration, and the list goes on.

There is an obvious truth, that damages done to democracy by this administration will affect Republicans, Democrats, and Independents, alike. In any case, our children and grandchildren will pay the price of lost freedoms and economic opportunity.

What is not so obvious is the deliberate attempt by both parties to split the American people into ever smaller, easier to control fractions. Part of the reason is the loss of common values, and rampant mistrust. Even the media, once regarded as the fourth leg of our government, the protector of freedoms, enjoys only 11% trust among the Millennials, and they are tech savvy. The big question remains. Why do we let the government and press, the least trusted people in the United States, tell us how to think, not only about each other, but to swallow propaganda about what a great job they are doing?

They have clearly demonstrated a total lack of managerial skill and refuse to take responsibility for their actions, with either, "I didn't know," "I wasn't responsible," "George did it," or "it has been broken for 50 years, as the Veterans Administration. If they do not know, and are not accountable, why do we, the people that hire them, not throw them out on their well-cushioned butts?

Business has become fair game for not investing stored up capital and creating more jobs. The answer is that everyone hoards or saves when facing uncertainty, in this case caused by unnecessary regulation and distrust. When the government acts without consequence, distrust levels rise accordingly. In our personal lives, faced with uncertainty, large unnecessary expenses are deferred as long as possible. That is smart money management. Only the government seems to be immune from spending sprees that jeopardize the economy.

The last and the most obvious observation are the implication that Americans lack a common value system. The United States once valued the rule of law, one that our government appears dedicated to repealing. I submit that this metrics indicates we all suffer the same frustrations and in general share the common values spelled out in the Declaration of Independence, the Constitution, and Bill of Rights.

Because some readers may be unfamiliar with, or forgotten the contents, following is the Declaration of Independence and the Bill of Rights.

The Declaration of Independence

IN CONGRESS, July 4, 1776.

The unanimous Declaration of the thirteen united States of America.

When in the Course of human events, it becomes necessary for one people to dissolve the political bands which have connected them with another, and to assume among the powers of the earth, the separate and equal station to which the Laws of Nature and of Nature's God entitle them, a decent respect to the opinions of mankind requires that they should declare the causes which impel them to the separation.

We hold these truths to be self-evident, that all men are created equal, that they are endowed by their Creator with certain unalienable Rights, that among these are Life, Liberty and the pursuit of Happiness.--That to secure these rights, Governments are instituted among Men, deriving their just powers from the consent of the governed, --That whenever any Form of Government becomes destructive of these ends, it is the Right of the People to alter or to abolish it, and to institute new Government, laying its foundation on such principles and organizing its powers in such form, as to them shall seem most likely to effect their Safety and Happiness. Prudence, indeed, will dictate that Governments long established should not be changed for light and transient causes; and accordingly all experience hath shewn, that mankind are more disposed to suffer, while evils are sufferable, than to right themselves by abolishing the forms to which they are accustomed. But when a long train of abuses and usurpations, pursuing invariably the same Object evinces a design to reduce them under absolute Despotism, it is their right, it is their duty, to throw off such Government, and to provide new Guards for their future security.--Such has been the patient sufferance of these Colonies; and such is now the necessity which constrains them to alter their former Systems of Government. The history of the present King of Great Britain is a history of repeated injuries and usurpations, all having in direct object the establishment of an absolute Tyranny over these States. To prove this, let Facts be submitted to a candid world.

The Bill of Rights

(The following is a transcription of the first ten amendments to the Constitution in their original form. These amendments were ratified December 15, 1791, and form what is known as the "Bill of Rights")

Amendment I

Congress shall make no law respecting an establishment of religion, or prohibiting the free exercise thereof; or abridging the freedom of speech, or of the press; or the right of the people peaceably to assemble, and to petition the Government for a redress of grievances.

Amendment II

A well-regulated Militia, being necessary to the security of a free State, the right of the people to keep and bear Arms, shall not be infringed.

Amendment III

No Soldier shall, in time of peace be quartered in any house, without the consent of the Owner, nor in time of war, but in a manner to be prescribed by law.

Amendment IV

The right of the people to be secure in their persons, houses, papers, and effects, against unreasonable searches and seizures, shall not be violated, and no Warrants shall issue, but upon probable cause, supported by Oath or affirmation, and particularly describing the place to be searched, and the persons or things to be seized.

Amendment V

No person shall be held to answer for a capital, or otherwise infamous crime, unless on a presentment or indictment of a Grand Jury, except in cases arising in the land or naval forces, or in the Militia, when in actual service in time of War or public danger; nor shall any person be subject for the same offence to be twice put in jeopardy of life or limb; nor shall be compelled in any criminal case to be a witness against himself, nor be deprived of life, liberty, or property, without due process of law; nor shall private property be taken for public use, without just compensation.

Amendment VI

In all criminal prosecutions, the accused shall enjoy the right to a speedy and public trial, by an impartial jury of the State and district wherein the crime shall have been committed, which district shall have been previously ascertained by law, and to be informed of the nature and cause of the accusation; to be confronted with the witnesses against him; to have compulsory process for obtaining witnesses in his favor, and to have the Assistance of Counsel for his defence.

Amendment VII

In Suits at common law, where the value in controversy shall exceed twenty dollars, the right of trial by jury shall be preserved, and no fact tried by a jury, shall be otherwise re-examined in any Court of the United States, than according to the rules of the common law.

Amendment VIII

Excessive bail shall not be required, nor excessive fines imposed, nor cruel and unusual punishments inflicted.

Amendment IX

The enumeration in the Constitution, of certain rights, shall not be construed to deny or disparage others retained by the people.

Amendment X

The powers not delegated to the United States by the Constitution, nor prohibited by it to the States, are reserved to the States respectively, or to the people.

There are additional amendments, but these form the original core of the Bill of Rights.

Summary

The people determine changes to the values for the country, spelled out in the Declaration of Independence, Constitution, and Bill of Rights. Although imperfect, these documents form a set of common values, and the debate over the meaning will continue, requiring functional and responsible legislative bodies and courts. Our elected officials are accountable for the enforcement of, and conforming to, the Constitution. The President and every member of Congress and the Senate take an oath promising to uphold the Constitution, and are not above the law. The ultimate betrayal by government is when officials use the mechanisms of law to promote themselves and/or ideals non-conforming to the will of the people.

Ultimately, the voters are responsible for the government, through actions at the ballot box. We vote politicians into office, and when they violate our trust, we must vote them out. While many Americans do not trust the process because it is tainted with big money or political chicanery, voting is one of two actions available. The other is getting involved in the process itself. We have the responsibility of performing due diligence, finding out the facts about the people and policies being voted on. Citizens reap the consequences for abdicating their responsibility to vote.

Our job is to roll up our sleeves, clean-up government, restore trust to our systems, and provide freedoms and opportunities to future generations.

OUR TURN

July, 2014 Issue 13

The 4th of July is a time to celebrate America, and the values it stands for, with flags flying, bands blaring out the National Anthem and fireworks exploding in the night sky.

Sorrow

Joy is elusive this year. This week, I attended the funeral for a veteran from the Vietnam era. Following the Catholic burial service, he received military recognition. The honor guard was impeccable in pressed Navy whites, with properly worn chrome helmets. Every action was precise, salutes sharp, arms straight. The barks of the M1 Garand's in the 21-gun salute were as one. The bugle player for Taps was older, and the music wavered slightly, but still reminiscent of the nights in the barracks and field. The music sadly floated over this warrior, as it has millions of others, a final farewell to arms. The honor guard folded the flag carefully and correctly into a triangle, and then reverently presented the symbol to his widow.

The ceremony recognized this veteran for deeds, not words, serving America honorably to preserve our values and system, as men and women have done since the American Revolution.

The funeral was a reminder of how our military is under attack. The bomb blasts are political and unheard or ignored by the media. Further, there is complicity by the American people, who vote clueless people into office, often ignorant or uncaring about the responsibilities of the military. Combined, these paradigms are degrading the most powerful force ever assembled for freedom, both politically and economically, in the history of humankind. Following is a summarization of key issues affecting our military. For these reasons, although citizens first and military second, they are unable to stand up and fight for their rights.

For those not privileged to serve, there are a few fundamental concepts to understand.

The Chain of Command

The military is a tightly organized hierarchy, titled the chain of command. To preserve order and focus on the battlefield, it is essential that all military personnel precisely follow orders communicated through this chain. Obviously, without controlled actions, chaos would ensue with every battle lost. The concept is programmed into every recruit until it is totally accepted, or the individual is discharged. Disobedience is unacceptable.

The President of the United States of America is the Commander-In-Chief of the military per the Constitution of the United States. There is no requirement for a president to have experience with, or knowledge about how the military functions.

Article II Section 2 of the U.S. Constitution, the Commander in Chief clause, states that "[t]he President shall be Commander in Chief of the Army and Navy of the United States, and of the Militia of the several States, when called into the actual Service of the United States."

The oath taken by military officers is:

> I, _____, having been appointed an officer in the Army of the United States, as indicated above in the grade of _____ do solemnly swear (or affirm) that I will support and defend the Constitution of the United States against all enemies, foreign and domestic, that I will bear true faith and allegiance to the same; that I take this obligation freely, without any mental reservations or purpose of evasion; and that I will well and faithfully discharge the duties of the office upon which I am about to enter; So help me God."

The oath taken by military enlisted personnel is:

> I, (*NAME*), do solemnly swear (or affirm) that I will support and defend the Constitution of the United States against all enemies, foreign and domestic; that I will bear true faith and allegiance to the same; and that I will obey the orders of the President of the United States and the orders of the officers appointed over me, according to regulations and the Uniform Code of Military Justice. So help me God.

71

In the military, what the President wants, the president gets. He/she is god, and has the power to make or break anyone in the service, or working for the government after discharge. Following are some of the measures instituted by the Obama Administration.

Purging the Military

Embroiled in the controversies of Benghazi, Fast and Furious, and misuse of the IRS, the Obama administration moved strongly to remove all sources they felt were unreliable to their message. First, Gen. David Petraeus, caught up in scandal, resigned as head of the CIA. A year later, President Obama fired nine senior commanding officers. Speculation is that he feared a strong military and purged any potential opposition to strategy, policy, or actions.

> Major General Michael Carey
> Vice Admiral Tim Giardina
> Lieutenant General David Holmes Huntoon, Jr.
> Major General C.M.M. Gurganus
> Major General Gregg A. Sturdevant
> Brigadier General Bryan Roberts
> Major General Ralph Baker
> Rear Admiral Charles Gaouette
> General Carter F. Ham

Three of these men were involved, directly or peripherally, during the Benghazi attack, Gen. Ham, Major General Baker, and Rear Admiral Gaouette. The reports on their reactions to on-going events vary, whether they supported attempting armed intervention, believed that we had response capability, or if a response was even possible. In Gen Ham's case, reports go in both directions. Some reports state he was in the process of over-riding the stand-down order and was subsequently relieved. In his testimony, he indicated that poorly positioned assets prevented a reaction. Remember, however, the military serves the Commander In Chief.

Altogether, the administration purged hundreds of officers, for a variety of reasons, real or implied. It has become obvious that if a military person speaks out, the response will be fast and harsh. The mainstream media essentially ignored these unprecedented events.

The purging of the military by the administration stands in stark contrast to the non-response taken on civilian issues. These include Fast and Furious, Benghazi, and political activism by governmental agencies like the IRS. In addition, the corruption in the Veterans Hospital systems, while not ignored, was softly addressed when it was time to take names, kick ass and take care of the veterans. The President and media ignored or minimized every controversial issue.

Rules of Engagement

The Rules of Engagement for Afghanistan, reestablished by President Obama, put our military in far greater danger than necessary. Our military is not comprised of killers and mercenaries, and our government must not put troops in indefensible positions.

Allen West, US Army Lt Colonel (Ret) and former member of the House of Representatives, on February 13, 2014, tweeted about the Rules of Engagement.

> "As a former combat commander, I can tell you that fear is difficult to avoid on the battlefield. But on today's battlefields, a new fear haunts our troops; the fear of persecution by their own government. That fear leads to hesitation, and that leads to death."

No man left behind

On 9/11/2012, terrorists attacked the U.S. consulate in Benghazi, Libya. Our government did nothing, leaving four people, including an Ambassador, to die during a preventable attack, which took place on a predictable date, 9-11. The President went to bed, requiring a good night's rest for a political fundraiser in Las Vegas the next day.

Reportedly, someone in his administration ordered a stand down to rescue attempts. Regardless, all those involved violated the protocol demanding action, even if it fails, to save Americans under attack.

Ignoring all lessons learned President Obama exchanged five terrorist leaders for Sgt. Bergdahl, an alleged deserter, thereby making him a hero. While done in the name of "leaving no man behind," a political stunt that immediately backfired.

Here are the names of the five Taliban commanders, the "Gitmo Five," released in exchange for Bergdahl. Classified as "high risk," all were collectively responsible for thousands of deaths, including Americans.

> Abdul Haq Wasiq
> Mullah Norullah Noori
> Mullah Mohammad Fazi
> Mullah Khairullah Khairkhwa
> Mohammad Nabi Omara.

Remember these names. They may well become the new Osama Bin Laden's, doing everything in their power to punish the evil enemy – the United States of America. The probability is high that Americans, both military and civilian, will die as a direct result of this trade. The irony is that politicians and press members chastise and condemn members of Bergdahl's unit, the same brothers in arms that tried to find and rescue him, some dying in the process.

Sgt. Andrew Tahmooressi has been in a Mexican jail since March 31, when he accidentally drove across a poorly marked U.S.-Mexico border. He had weapons and ammunition in the car, and reportedly suffers from PTSD. The President, at least outwardly, has done nothing to free this American left behind. In the meantime, thousands of illegal immigrants have crossed the border into the United States, some carrying guns, other smuggling drugs, and/or people.

The Veterans Administration

On this very day, our wounded comrades across the country are still fighting for medical care from our bloated, bureaucratic Veterans Administration. Every citizen in the United States, by virtue of having military protection, commits to providing them quality health care. Some of our military were on lists to receive medical care, and those lists later destroyed. Our government, of both parties, seems unwilling to mount the effort to search out each person with deferred treatment or appointments, and then break every speed record to provide medical attention. Of all the failures, the VA debacle is one of the most preventable and tragic. It is unconscionable that veterans die or suffer, while Congress dawdles and the President plays another round of golf, both protected by fabulous health care systems.

Join Navy and Marine Corps veteran Montel Williams in his intense, angry, social media campaign to get President Obama, and Congress to act immediately to fix the VA. Simply appointing a new administrator will not get the job done.

The Long List

This newsletter only touches the surface of issues affecting our military, but the ones covered make the point. Our military is in a tough position, and nothing on the horizon appears to improve the situation. Certainly, no one wants a reason, like war, to improve conditions. The reality is, we are currently at war in Afghanistan, and radical Islam is at war with us, even if our government chooses to ignore it. We still live in a dangerous world and need an active and energized military to protect the homeland and sometimes-undeserving citizenry.

Our military is the protector from tyranny, the powerful force of men and women standing against dangers both domestic and foreign, which are hell-bent on reducing us to third world status, then slitting our throats. Recognized or not, our freedoms and military are under attack, and have been for nearly six years.

This is for my brothers and sisters in arms, all in lockstep though the march of time, from the Continental Army to present. We pay tribute to those still living who served in the World Wars, Korea, Vietnam, Desert Storm, Iraq, and Afghanistan and in between. Not all served on the firing line, but each made a difference, and none is diminished. All stood ready to fight for the equal rights and freedoms of all Americans, even those who would deny those very rights.

Say a prayer for all of our comrades, who are broken in body or mind. They paid a high price for our right to practice the religion of our choice, and criticize our leaders without fear of consequences. Pray for all of our brothers and sisters still in harm's way. All have paid the price in blood and treasure for the freedoms that make America the land of opportunity, a unique place where dreams can come true, no matter how humble our origins. Pray for the safety and well-being of all those who stand in defense of this great nation, still the world's greatest land of opportunity.

In the old Western movies, just as the enemy starts to win, the Cavalry rides in to save the day. Our job as citizens and veterans is to be the Cavalry for our active military, unable for many reasons to speak up and fight for themselves. It is our turn to defend them. Honor and duty bind us to that moral purpose.

Epilogue

Sgt. Tahmooressi was released on Nov 1, 2014. Montel Williams and Greta Van Susteren deserve a great deal of credit. They both maintained constant pressure on politicians, the media, and legal representation. President Obama never raised a finger to make sure "no soldier was left behind."

In this case, the press gets an A+. A marine (Montel) and newsperson (Van Susteren) combined to positive purpose and facilitated his release. Without their relentless work and pressure on elected officials and other influential persons, Sgt. Tahmooressi would still be in prison, undergoing torture by his captors.

76

Sgt. Bergdahl

The military has completed its investigation into the circumstance surrounding Sgt. Bergdahl abduction or desertion, but has not made the findings public.

Speaking out

I am happily wrong about the military taking a passive role.

Former Secretary of Defense Robert M. Gates challenged President Obama's commitment to the Afghan War in his book "Duty: Memoirs of a Secretary of War."

Former Secretary of Defense Leon Panetta published a new book, titled "Worthy Fights: A Memoir of Leadership in War and Peace".

> A book excerpt in Time Magazine recounts the internal battles over the timing of the withdrawal of U.S. troops from Iraq and whether a residual force would remain. Panetta and other Pentagon officials argued for keeping that force.

> "My fear, as I voiced to the President and others," Panetta writes, "was that if the country split apart or slid back into the violence that we'd seen in the years immediately following the U.S. invasion, it could become a new haven for terrorists to plot attacks against the U.S." He adds that his stance "reflected not just my views but also those of the military commanders in the region and the Joint Chiefs."

The military told the Obama administration precisely what would happen if America pulled all of our military assets out of Iraq.

Following is an excerpt from Chicago Magazine.

> Worthy Fights: A Memoir of Leadership in War and Peace contains a surprisingly harsh assessment of President Obama, whom

77

Panetta <u>describes</u> as having "lost his way," particularly on foreign policy. Panetta notes Obama's weak leadership, "reticence to engage his opponents," ignoring his own chemical-weapons "red line" in Syria, neglecting to arm the Syrian rebels, and failing to push hard enough for a residual force in Iraq. The result, writes Panetta, is the horror of ISIS. Panetta's memoir is so harsh in places that it makes <u>Bob Gates' memoir</u>, released earlier this year—Gates was Panetta's predecessor as secretary of defense—look somewhat milder in its takedown of Obama as Commander in Chief.www.chicagomag.com/Chicago-Magazine/Felsenthal-Files/October-2014/Leon-Panetta-Scorches-Obama-Praises-Rahm-in-New-Memoir/

These are historical critiques of a sitting president by past cabinet members. The good news is they are speaking out. The bad news is we have a weak, disrespected Commander in Chief of the most powerful military in history. Compounding the problem, our country is slowly being drawn, Vietnam like, back into a combat role in Iraq.

The Veterans Administration

The new head of the Veterans Administration, Secretary McDonald, is taking action to restructure the organization, but progress is slow. Although criminal acts were probably committed, no charges were filed.

Taps

A Marine brother-in-arms has marched into God's arms. His fellow marines gave him full accord, the haunting sound of taps, a folded flag for the widow, and a twenty-one gun salute. Dennis Groshek was a friend, brother-in-law, and a staunch American. He did not live long enough to see the rejection of President Obama's policies in the 2014 election, but he must be celebrating in Heaven. His beloved freedom-loving America still has a chance. We will all miss him.

Harvey Staley, a veteran of the Korean conflict, joined the ranks marching to God's eternal cadence.

THE CHILDREN IMMIGRANTS

August, 2014 Issue 14

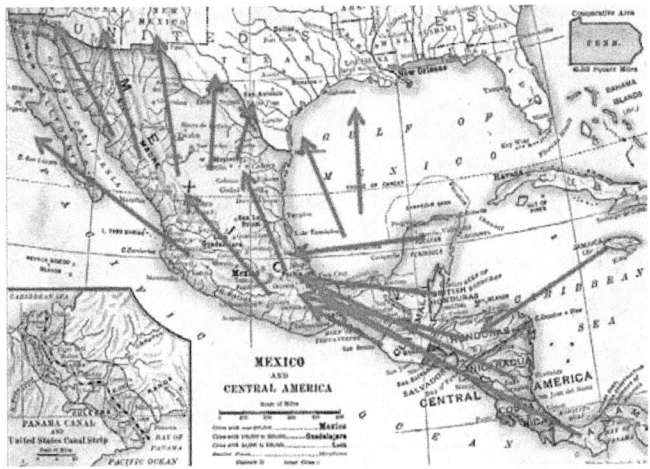

The Problem

Today, tens of thousands of undocumented immigrants, many unaccompanied children, illegally surge over the US/Mexican border, and then surrender to the border patrol. The masses are multi-sourced, from the Caribbean, Central America, and other countries. The trip is perilous, made possible by organized criminals and corrupted officials, who welcome two additional revenue streams. These are extremely violent people, with little regard for life, who use and abuse the children. The criminals make money by funneling the immigrants through Mexico and across the border, but also by supplying the sex trade across the world with untraceable young women. Although the latter circumstance is undocumented, having some knowledge of the border, and recognizing that crime seizes every opportunity, be sure it occurs. Predators never let a tender prey escape. The immigrants provide a shield, distracting the border patrol, while criminals more easily smuggle drugs into the United States. There are reports that the physical and sexual abuse continues in the crowded refugee centers.

They come for many reasons, primarily opportunities for a new and better life in America, enabled and encouraged by conditions created by the Obama administration. The problem is not the children, who must be provided safety and with compassionate concern for their current and future welfare. We must find a way to provide them hope or at least options. These include return to their home countries, or finding families in America.

A secondary issue is health related. The immigrants are mostly untested for transmittable diseases, yet our government is distributing them across the country, setting the stage for potential epidemics.

Obviously, the opportunity is ripe for enemies to infiltrate our borders, and the probability is very high they are doing exactly that.

Root Cause

The root cause of the fiasco is a commitment made by candidate Barack Obama to the Latino community in 2008. He promised them a comprehensive immigration bill to provide a pathway to citizenship.

The Latino vote was 67 percent for Obama. Without their vote, John McCain would have been the new president. In President Obama's first term, given both a Democratic Senate and Congress, comprehensive legislation was a near guarantee, but the president reneged on his promise.

Running for office a second time in 2012, faced with the potential loss of Latino voters and a recalcitrant Republican majority in the House, Obama issued a directive, not technically an executive order, through then-Secretary of Home Land Security, Janet Napolitano. Dated June 15, 2012, she issued the "Dream Act," providing a pathway for the children of immigrants born in America. Technically, it was a directive to ignore current laws in contrast to alternate legislation, but served the same purpose. In 2012, nine percent of all votes cast were from the Latino community, and 71 percent voted for Obama, assuring his re-election.

Obviously, the strategy worked but it laid the foundation for the current crisis at the border.

Many of the immigrants believe they will automatically become citizens, with all the benefits accrued to that status, when they reach America.

Border Towns

Even given the fuzzy, illogical promise, I wondered how parents could send their children into harm's way, and then recalled my own experiences. Nothing has changed. Desperate people do what others may consider unreasonable.

It helps to have some understanding of border towns. Survival in resource-poor circumstances requires changing people's lives, priorities, and perspective, some for the better, others for the worse. To that purpose, here are two personal experiences.

At seventeen, in the military and undergoing surgical technician training at Fort Sam Houston Medical center in San Antonio, Texas, a group of us drove through the desert to Nuevo Laredo, Mexico, across the border from Laredo, Texas. We checked into our hotel and went to a restaurant, where young prostitutes immediately started hitting on us. Throughout the evening, as we bar hopped, this naive boy from southern Kansas was shocked at the open, ongoing parade of sex, alcohol, and drugs.

Years later, I was assigned to conduct the annual inventory audit at the Nogales, Mexico plant. I flew into Tucson, AZ on Saturday, rented a car, and drove to the assigned desert resort. Before leaving home, I promised my wife to attend Mass if possible. I drove to the border, parked on the American side and walked across the Rio Grande Bridge, into Nogales. There was an old Catholic Church in the square, and the sign stated that Mass started in roughly an hour. While it was early dusk, the Mariachi music signaled that downtown was open for action. After sitting for a while, a middle-aged man approached, and we spoke for a few minutes. Then he said, "My daughter, she is a virgin, and I can make her available to you." Married with four children, and more knowledgeable about human behavior, I simply said, "no thank you." The conversation over, he lit the candles on the altar, and when Mass began, he was the Acolyte.

The next day at the plant, I approached the topic with the Plant Manager, an American, and the accountant, a Mexican.

The plant manager replied, "When you have zero other assets, and you are hungry and probably have other mouths to feed, you sell thirty minutes of your daughter's time. Food, water, and a place to live carry greater value, and sex is an exchangeable, renewable, and marketable asset."

The accountant said, "You would be amazed at how many families send their girls to the border cities, to work as prostitutes. They save enough money and return home to get married. In many cases, girls are sold into the trade against their wills. It seems strange to you, a person with many available choices, but you do not have the right to judge people living in these circumstances. You can only try to understand how limited their options are."

I returned home better informed but feeling less human. I could not imagine in my wildest nightmare, with three daughters, how parents could do this. However, today, thousands send their children into the jaws of this horrible, monstrous system, where they may simply disappear forever.

The Desert

If the immigrants survive slavery and abuse, the next step is a hostile trip to the border across a scorching desert, by bus, packed in hot trucks, or by foot. Many will die, reclaimed by the coyotes, crows, and rodents. Their parents will never know where they are, or if they are deceased, only mourn their loss, knowing they may have contributed. The following map shows the entire 1,933 miles of the border separating the United States and Mexico.

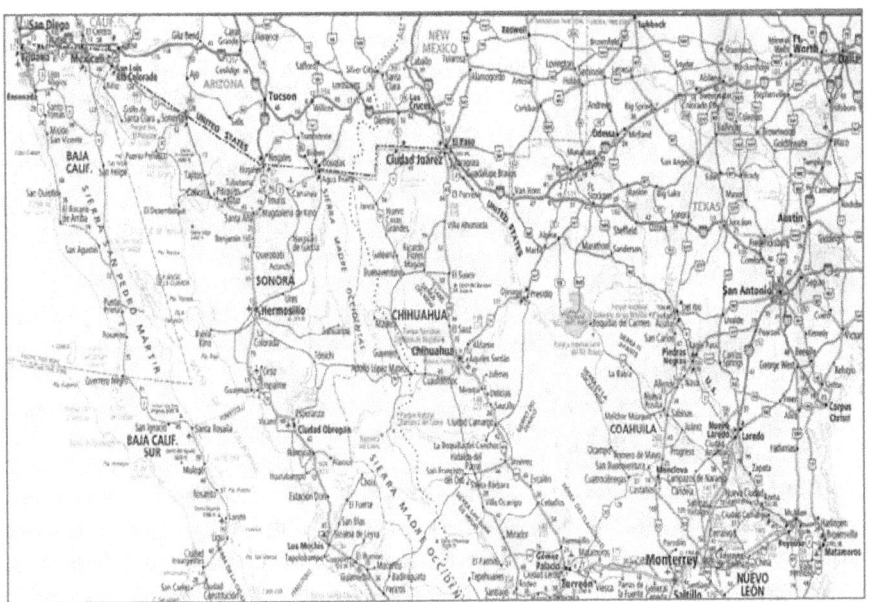

In 2002, I drove to California, expecting to start a project, and while there, heard about people trying to cross the border. The project was delayed for several months so I decided to drive back to Wisconsin. As a photographer and analyst, and curious as usual, the decision was made to drive home via Mexico, a circuitous route, but more interesting than the interstate highway system. Against all advice, the selected route was to Douglas, AZ, entering Mexico, and driving east on Highway 2, to El Paso, TX via Ciudad Juarez, Mexico. (Google Maps shows the distance at 240 miles, and estimates slightly less than six hours to complete. It proved to be a very enlightening trip, lasting nearly nine hours).

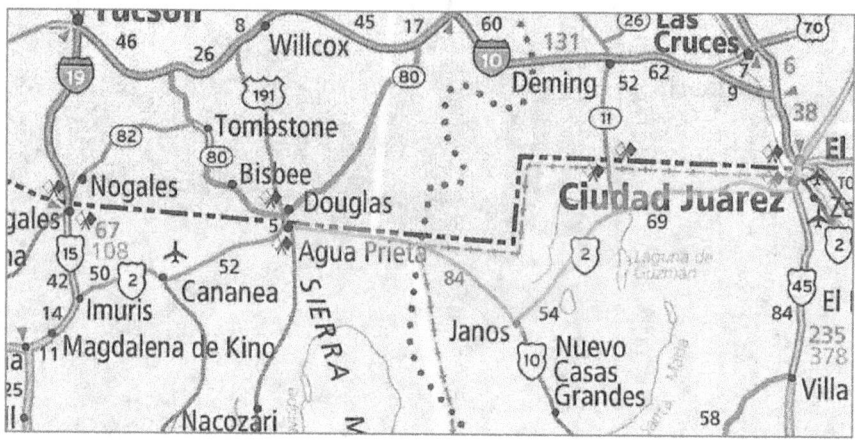

The entire trip, through the Sonoran desert, with the sun beating down, was very hot, and I ran the air-conditioning intermittently. Once, concerned about overheating in dangerous circumstances, I turned on the heater to cool the engine. The route was mostly dry scrub desert, but it was too dangerous to stop and photograph.

There were small areas with roughly constructed buildings, even cardboard shanties, and people of all ages walking around. About half way through the trip, with less distance from the road to the border, these shantytowns were quite large, stretching for miles. They were staging areas for destitute people with one objective, to cross the Rio Grande and enter the United States. Today, these shantytowns must be much more extensive.

Driving past these shantytowns, with children, women and rough looking men watching, I felt very vulnerable, a huge resource rich fish, traveling just a little too fast to harvest. Taking photographs was out of the question. To make matters worse, arriving in Juarez, I discovered the normal route to the bridge crossing the border closed, and was soon lost on dirt back roads. Coming to a paved street, there were a number of brightly dressed people gathering. I asked three teen-agers, hoping they would know English, what was happening and asked how to get back to the bridge. They said it was Saturday night, when people dressed up and enjoyed the company of their neighbors. They provided directions back to the right route, and the safely of Texas, United States of America.

It would be unthinkable to try this trip today, across areas controlled by drug cartels, coyotes smuggling people, and Juarez is one of the murder capitals of the world.

The Hard Road to Perceived Opportunity

Returning to California later in the year, most of the associates in the plant were Latino. One, I'll call him Juan, was a tough looking guy who loves America, perhaps with greater intensity than most born here. His story was harrowing. He and his sister were from the Dominican Republic, where their father was a ranking member of the government. Juan and his sister were pro-freedom dissidents against that same government. One night, with an arrest warrant out for his children, Juan's father gave them airline tickets to Mexico. Juan was sixteen, and his sister only fourteen. They spent nearly two harrowing years, with

Juan repeatedly and violently protecting his sister, before illegally entering the United States. They both received citizenship under President Reagan's amnesty program.

Responsibility

Regardless of how the Obama administration tries to spin the story, the President, and his executive pen, created this cruel situation. He knew for two years it was in process, (from the time of the Dream Directive), but he did nothing to stop it, even enabling the situation. He hoped to shame the Republicans into passing comprehensive legislation. When the media started showing the children in make shift camps, President Obama shut down the area and prevented coverage, ignoring the concept of a free press, a different but troubling topic. The administration even barred members of congress from the facilities. Obviously, the entire situation is a brutal travesty of governance and responsibility.

The administration has asked the legislative branch for 3.7 billion dollars to respond to a crisis they created, and that brings the problem squarely home in other extremely profound ways.

President Obama is spending greater amounts of money for the new arrivals, at the expense of millions of young Americans. The immigrants will have better prospects than citizens trapped in poor economic situations. Where do American parents send their children to find opportunities?

Of all the devious uncaring actions taken by this administration, none is quite as callous as this one, trading off the future of our children to achieve the political objective of keeping the Latino community in the Democratic Party. Coupled with the fiasco of failing on veteran's health care, and 4.8 million abortions during his tenure, the President exhibits little concern for life, unless the loss directly affects his poll numbers and/or legacy.

The entire situation has deeply diminished and blemished our great country. Tears of shame should cascade from every American eye, as we comprehend the corrupted situation surrounding the world's most valuable asset, the children.

Epilogue

February 12, 2014

Megan Kelly, on Fox News, interviewed Jonathan Turley, a Washington University Law School professor.

> "What I'm hearing certainly causes great concern that he (President Obama) will again violate the separation of powers. No president can take on the power of all three branches and that's what he seems to be doing. He certainly seems to be taking on legislative authority. He isn't being particularly coy about this, you know he says 'this is what I wanted to get out of legislation and I'm going to do it on my own' and that does become a government of one.

> It's a very sad moment but it's becoming a particularly dangerous moment if the president is going to go forward, particularly after this election to defy the will of Congress yet again. I can understand the frustration, these are two political parties that cannot get along but as you said, we have a Democratic process and a Congress that's coming in with the full voice of the American people behind them, that's what an election is, you may disagree with the outcome, but you have to respect the outcome. What the President is suggesting is tearing at the very fabric of the constitution. We have a separation of powers that gives us balance and that doesn't protect the branches. It's not there to protect the executive branch or the legislative branch, it's there to protect liberty. It's there to keep any branch from assuming so much control that they become a threat to liberty.

I always tell my friends on the Democratic side, we will rue the day when we helped create this uber presidency," he said. "What the Democrats are creating is something very very dangerous. They're creating a president who can go at it alone and to go at it alone is something that is a very danger that the framers sought to avoid in our constitution."

On February 26, 2014, Jonathan Turley testified before Congress. Following is an excerpt from his presentation. The full text is available at http://jonathanturley.files.wordpress.com/2014/02/turley-enforcement-testimony.pdf

I highly recommend anyone concerned about liberty, and the interpretation of the intent of the framers, to read the entirety of this extremely sobering presentation.

"Enforcing the President's Constitutional Duty to Faithfully Execute the Laws"

"I recently testified before this Committee on the history and function of the separation of powers in our system. I also discussed how, in my view, President Obama has repeatedly violated this doctrine in the circumvention of Congress in areas ranging from health care to immigration law to environmental law. I will not repeat that discussion here because this hearing is not about the existence of such violations but the possible corrective measures that can be taken in light of those violations.

Given the issues at stake in this debate, it is vital that we speak plainly about the current conflicts between the Executive Branch and the Legislative Branch. We are in the midst of a constitutional crisis with sweeping implications for our system of government. There has been a massive gravitational shift of authority to the Executive Branch that threatens the stability and functionality of our tripartite system. To be sure, this shift did not begin with President Obama. However, it has accelerated at an alarming rate under this Administration.

These changes are occurring in a political environment with seemingly little oxygen for dialogue, let alone compromise. Indeed, the current anaerobic conditions are breaking down the muscle of the constitutional system that protects us all. Of even greater concern is the fact that the other two branches appear passive, if not inert, as the Executive Branch has assumed such power.

As someone who voted for President Obama and agrees with many of his policies, it is often hard to separate the ends from the means of presidential action. Indeed, despite decades of thinking and writing about the separation of powers, I have had momentary lapses where I privately rejoiced in seeing actions on goals that I share, even though they were done in the circumvention of Congress. For example, when President Obama unilaterally acted on greenhouse gas pollutants, I was initially relieved. I agree entirely with the priority that he has given this issue. However, it takes an act of willful blindness to ignore that the greenhouse regulations were implemented only after Congress rejected such measures and that a new sweeping regulatory scheme is now being promulgated solely upon the authority of the President.

We are often so committed to a course of action that we conveniently dismiss the means as a minor issue in light of the goals of the Administration. Many have embraced the notion that all is fair in love and politics. However, as I have said too many times before Congress, in our system it is often more important how we do something than what we do. Priorities and policies (and presidents) change. What cannot change is the system upon which we all depend for our rights and representation."

Jonathon Turley is a tower in the legal profession and one of the most brilliant legal thinkers of our time. In addition, he has the courage to speak up. Attempting to add to his commentary would be equivalent of attempting to modify $E=mc^2$.

Mr. Turley would make an excellent Supreme Court Justice. The primary qualification is not political party; it is adherence to the rule of law and embracing liberty. His website is Jonathanturley.org.

OF COWS AND CATTLE

September, 2014 Issue 15

There will be two September Focused Fire Newsletters. The scheduled issue is still in process, but the deadline for the newsletter is now. Visiting a farm, our youngest adult daughter inadvertently provided a solution of how to meet the deadline and have a little fun. She had some interesting snapshots of cows, but one photograph really stood out. It represented an opportunity to poke some fun at our government. When asked if I could use the photo, her first response was "yes." Given further details on content, she declared they were just cute innocent cows, and the photograph was not available for political purposes.

Now emotionally committed to a humorous interim newsletter, I took a series of photographs, serving the purpose while allowing her cows and superior photos to retain their integrity. Perhaps she will share the very cool photograph on Facebook.

The Three branches of Government

Embedded Czars
Do it to'ers

public trough

Executive	Judicial	Legislative
"Mooer"	"Chewer"	"Pooper"

BUT NO DOER

Something stinks? Is it still the economy, or what?

I've got a pen and
I've got a phone.

The barriers are just too big. No way we can get anything done.

You call them blood sucking flies

I call them lobbyists

The Herd

We the citizens and taxpayers keep voting the same
politicians into office, and they never fail to disappoint.
Pogo was right. "We has met the enemy, and he is us!"

COMING SOON - A NATIONAL DATA BASE OF YOU

September, 2014 Issue 16

Information is a tool for great good or evil, depending on how and who uses it. It is critical to understand that information is the new currency of global exchange. Governments, industry, and individuals spend billions of dollars in search of every type of information. Our personal data is our most valuable and highly sought-after possession. It directly links to our wealth and personal power. Every citizen of the United States, and most of the world, is in danger of losing personal freedoms by the misappropriation or misapplication of their invisible data self.

 As consultants, we are information management professionals and understand how close it resides to the power apex. The more actionable data one has, the greater the opportunity to create information and take advantage of people, turning situations to our cause or profit. Information is the competitive edge, enabling every type of physical action or reaction. This applies to all of society, personal relationships, health care, business competition, politics, and government. Please note the distinction between politics and government because later in this Newsletter, the difference is quite relevant.

This newsletter explores the cause and consequences of the rapidly merging information databases, potentially into a National Database of You and Me. We will develop a personal database model and merge it into hypothetical information. These data are useful to manipulate or coerce us into taking action against our free will, or for the greater good as defined for an idealistic objective with which we may not agree.

It is useful to establish a base of definitions. Data equates to fragments of, or complete facts, that on their own may be insignificant. Data is analog, or digital, and may be numeric, letters, or image. Data are calculated, correlated, and analyzed.

95

Metadata is data that describes data. Date and time stamps on photography, type, size of an image, when and where the image was created, are metadata. Another example is the time, location, caller, and recipient of a cell telephone call.

A database is a collection of data organized, stored, and indexed, and accessed using multiple types of algorithms and program languages and other access tools. For example, Query optimization. Following is a hierarchal structure for an average person. Inquiries are possible from any piece of data.

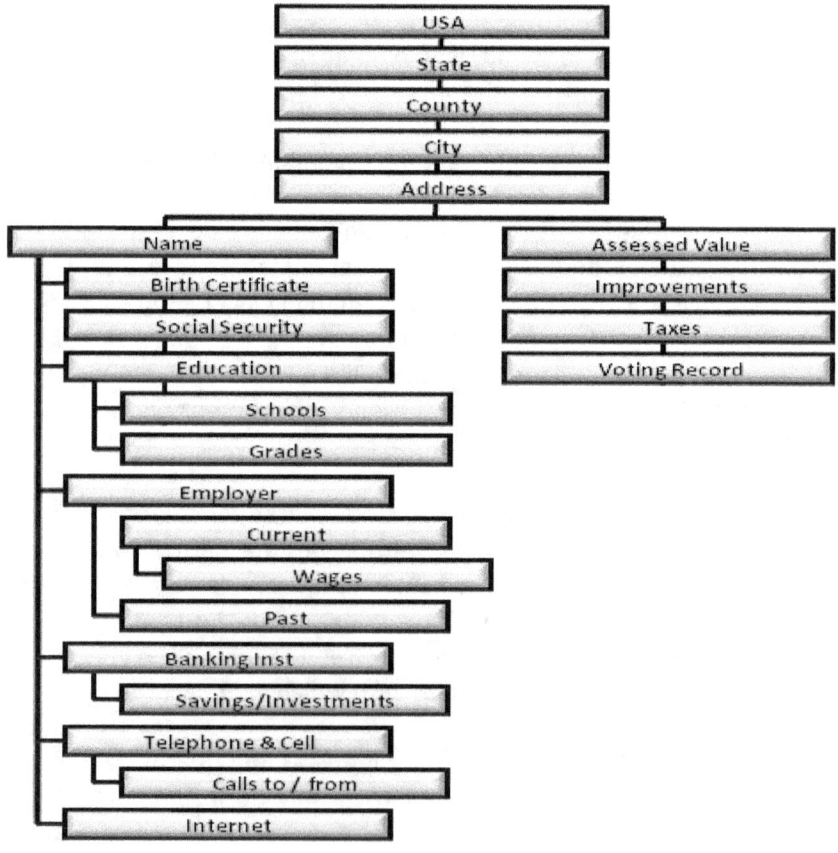

In theory, everyone contributes to a database, and everyone accesses it for information. The internet and Google are good examples. In the real world, not everyone has equal access to the information in databases, and there are no controls over where it resides. Actually, using the cloud, information may exist in pieces on disparate computer systems anywhere in the world. Information is knowledge.

Information is the result of putting data into a useful form, or product. Your home address, for example, is data, but combined with city and state, it is a precise identifiable location.

While information was available in some form prior to the computer age, communicating it was relatively slow. Consistent with Moore's Law (transistor speed and power, e.g. computers, will double every two years); the information world today is pervasive, with a myriad of devices capturing and processing data of every type. The second part of the computing power equation is bandwidth or internet speed. Businesses and individuals have the ability to transmit large volumes of data/information anywhere in the world, and/or interact with business and each other in real-time.

Mobile technology has moved the information reality from the office to the world, from voice to image and text, from status to content rich streaming flows. Actionable information is real-time and social media such as Facebook or Linked-In enables global collaboration. The differences between hand-held devices and PCs are increasingly blurred, separated more by personal choice and ease of use than functionality. Miniaturized cameras, incorporated in multiple devices, enable the proliferation of images. The technologies as applied to business or personal applications are equally pervasive.

The commercial world

The consumer world has changed, with more of the action moving to the Internet. Business-to-customer (B2C) and business-to-business (B2B) applications are escalating. On-line sales of products on Black Monday, free of shipping costs, show annual growth greater than 15%. Every

97

transaction on the internet leaves a traceable footprint back to the buyer. These footprints are collected as both real data, such as purchase orders, names, bank codes, etc., and metadata.

Collectively, these create a condition labeled "big data." Retailers, government, and health care organizations are capturing large volumes of real-time data from multiple sources, including enterprise, vendors, patients, and customers. Where the prior evolutions of technology left business and government searching for viable analytical data, the problem today is how to manage and convert these large data into useful information products.

Big data requires massive storage capacity and easy access from anywhere in the world. It is not realistic to carry a computer with enough storage to conduct business and personal affairs. As individuals, we have big data problems as real to our situations as they are to business and governmental organizations. We also want access to every database available, for our own use and advantage. The cloud serves the purpose.

Enterprises of every type are working on integration and automation in some form. There may be opportunities for sharing solutions, especially in the arena of information technology. One example is Customer Relationship Management (CRM).

CRM was an early tool of Internet retailers, capturing real, and metadata from customer inquiries/purchases. The system tracks specifics - what they buy/sell/want or do not want, e-mail addresses, demographics, communications, event monitoring, project management, and collaboration programs. The information forms an accessible, real-time database useful for mining information, providing event alerts and analytical summarization. The database legislated in the Affordable Care Act (ACA), will potentially capture medical data in similar, if not greater, detail.

CRM data models predict and influence buying behavior. Practitioners call the systems "the voice of the customer." Every major retailer and many manufacturing enterprises utilize these systems. CRM technology has spread to other industries. One could argue about its intrusion into personal privacy, but CRM is a great processor for managing and analyzing large volumes of detailed information. The system has the potential to become Patient Relationship Processing because of its relational nature. This database of accurate information would be invaluable.

Mining for strategic, tactical, and individual purposes, facilitated by structured data, makes information accessible globally in real time via mobile technology.

The cloud

Cloud computing, a misnomer but a useful term, defines storage and processing solutions. Gartner defines cloud computing as "a style of computing in which scalable and elastic IT-enabled capabilities are delivered as a service using Internet technologies." Cloud service providers have massive or shared computer power and storage, paid for by subscription or amount of service used. These include multi-tenant service bureaus, and all web based processing, such as Software as a Service (SaaS), Service Oriented Architecture (SOA), and Application Service Provider (ASP), under the cloud umbrella.

The tools exist to integrate most systems and databases. The issue is cost, time, and result. The problems are the differences in format, field sizes, formulas used, programming language, and database technology. Each system is dissimilar in size and calculation, and conversion is required to move data back and forth from one system to the other. The reconciliation of these issues is basic to any form of automated integration, but the mashed result may introduce greater error than its parts.

Software code, defining how data will be processed and put into useful information, is relatively static. Modifications can be complicated and expensive. The term flexible information system means a set of tightly designed and written procedures for executing repetitive formulas, with designed-in flexibility through coding structures and functionality. Contemporary systems are much more adaptive, with Apps of virtually every type.

Analytics or intelligent software employing artificial intelligence, expert knowledge or other mathematics based computer models tap the power of the database. Enterprises of all types, including governments at every level have embraced the use of analytics, or intelligence tools. These come in a variety of sizes and shapes from simple drill down to complex analytics. The objective is to have functionality that builds information products-visualization, decision support, sales analysis, etc. in a timely and trustworthy fashion.

There are thousands of databases capturing and storing information on every type of activity. Of prime concern to this paper are the IRS, health care records, the browsing history on Google and other search engines, and the emergence of powerful and extremely useful geographic tools.

While this paper focuses primarily on the negative aspects of large integrated databases, some types of large systems are necessities. Comprehensive geo-information systems such as ESRI will insure our future survival. ESRI stands for Environmental Systems Research Institute.

ERSI is the most comprehensive geo-information company in the world. Their products are Geographic Information Systems (GIS), and geo database management applications. They can literally map the world and every feature about it, by fractions of an inch, for land use applications.

For more information, visit www.esri.com.

Following is a map of Ventura, CA, showing a precise location.

100

Like Google, from this specific location, the house and streets are identifiable. Unlike Google, these geophysical databases also contain the underground infrastructure and data needed to maintain the streets, fireplugs, electrical service, natural gas, cable television, etc. Tied to local tax data, these databases provide a comprehensive representation of the people living in the home, the value of the home, its construction, lot size- in other words, not just images but relevant information.

Extending the concept even further, farmers can literally obtain an inch-by-inch visualization and analysis of soil content. Using high-technology equipment, production optimization occurs for each inch. This involves the precise application of fertilizer and other soil enhancers, along with precise amounts of water as needed. (See the Advanced Agriculture presentation of CompetitiveAmerica.us). The technology has enormous benefits for managing natural and renewable resources. The functionally will enable huge gains in agricultural yields, warn us of geophysical problems, and help plan and execute optimal transportation routes. Geo information is also gathered and used to increase harvest and conservation of ocean resources. Human

101

imagination, creativity, and innovation are the only limits to the applications.

The problem, merging disparate databases multiples the potential for mischief, larceny, and coercion.

Health Care

The Affordable Care Act (ACA) demands the creation of a de facto national health care database. While it does not necessarily include personal health care data, in conformity with HIPAA 5010, it is comprised of codes and metadata. EMR/EHR records form an enormous share of the new quality standard in the ACA, and the completion of electronic records establishes the base for compensation.

5010 lays the foundation for ICD-10, a coding and classification system integral to the ACA. The purpose is to increase granularity for analytical purposes, but they expand the level of detail/complexity in coding and billing. There are two different sets. Codes for services, (CPT), and diagnoses (ICD-9). Other countries have already adopted ICD-10.

Number of Old Codes	
CPT	3,824
ICD-9	14,025
Total	17,849
Number of New Codes	
ICD-10	68,000
ICD-10-PCS	72,600
Total	140,600
Increase	122,751
Percent increase	688%

"Understanding ICD-10 and ICD-10-PC" Mary Jo Bowie and Regina Schaffer

Health care facilities must convert the old ICD-9 codes, which use a different format, into ICD-10-CM, a monumental data conversion application.

The inability to convert electronic records accurately indicates the quality issues associated with managing this volume of data. Setting up and maintaining accurate databases are an enormous effort at both the facility and federal levels. The cost will be staggering.

Every person receiving medical care will have services and conditions recorded in broad and extensive detail. Its use represents a two-edged sword. Striking with one edge, data will be available to help manage health care quality and focus on emerging issues. The federal governing board will use these data for service level decisions. Decisions on health care will be statistical and discriminate against certain medical conditions where the cost may not justify life-supporting treatment. In these cases, the sword slices the other direction.

Distribution analyses are fundamental tools for quality management. The greater the population of factors, the higher the number of variables, increasing the number of built in statistical errors. A patient unfortunate enough to have incorrect codes applied may get the wrong, or no treatment at all. Bad data will skew automated decisions. While this is true today, the mathematical explosion of errors inherent with multiplying the possibilities by 688% will worsen the problem proportionally. A shortage of qualified coders will potentially produce a highly inaccurate database.

The major concern in any application is data accuracy. The old acronym, GIGO, or garbage in, garbage out, has frightening implications for patient care.

Medical personnel created your information clone when they filled out your birth certificate. The data piled up geometrically, with education records, athletic and scholastic awards, newspapers, a brand new social security number, jobs, military record, business affiliations, tax records, internet surfing practices, where you worked, and how long, and sometimes even personal performance. In recent years, postings on Facebook, and other social media - literally any digital and savable information added to the compilations.

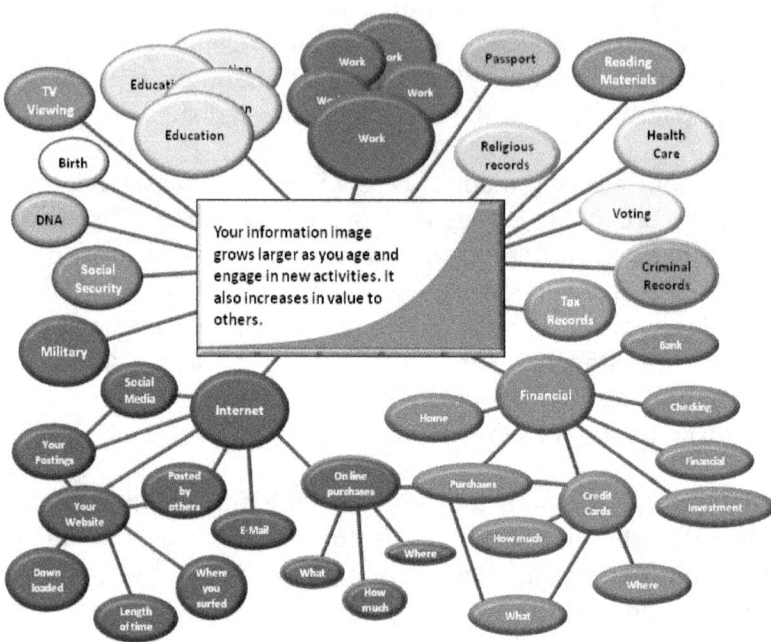

When we marry, our database suddenly increases, and the data for each member added to that of all the others.

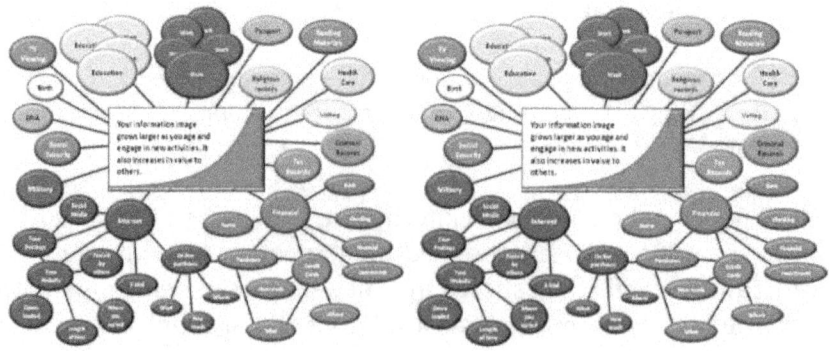

Each child further expands the database.

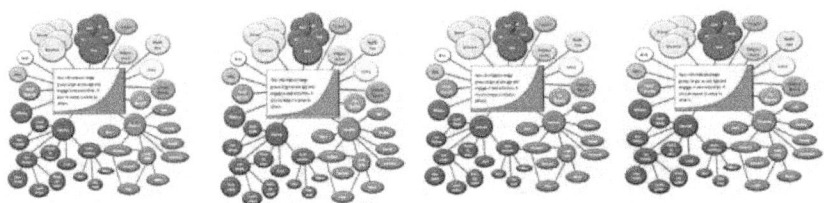

Nearly all stores, of all types, record and digitize every movement, and there are cameras on many streets. People randomly (or knowingly) take our photographs in virtually every environment, and given the size and stealth characteristics of recording equipment, we will never know it. Devices are available to track our cars, and to record every word uttered at work.

Currently, a tremendous amount of accumulated data exists about you and those you care for. It is located in an unknown number of disparate databases. The current situation targets everyone with commercial information including suggested purchases, and political messaging. In truth, everyone is subject to highly intrusive privacy violations increasing the data collected about you. Remarkably, even if we live a pure, boring, mundane life and never worry about blackmail, loved ones around us may not be clean-living and more subject to outside influence.

Right now, these converging computer technologies provide the data to build information capable of knowing where we are (cell phones), what we are buying (credit card transactions), and sometimes where we are going (Facebook, trip planning on Google or MapQuest). Even in your home, there can be embedded technology in your telephone, computer, television, automobile, or any device using computer chips. It is given that identity theft is pervasive, and we covered this topic in the April Focused Fire Newsletter, Issue 10, posted on CompetitiveAmerica.us and titled "Internet Security and Identity Theft." Unfortunately, this is only the beginning of the mischief possible when the databases are integrated.

This chart illustrates the current situation.

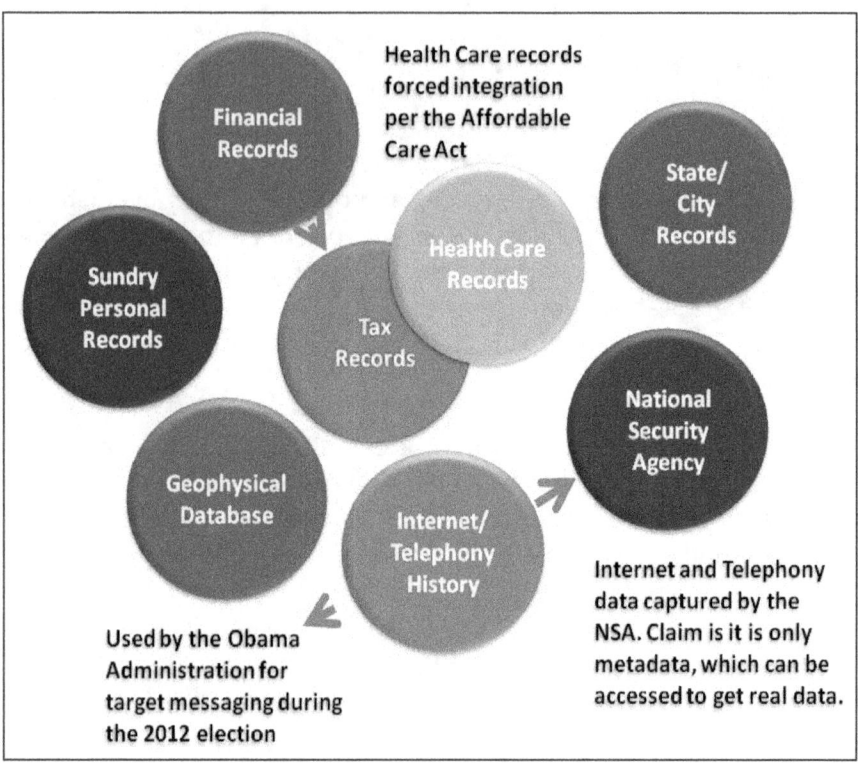

The integration of our health care records into the IRS database is part of the Affordable Care Act, fulfilling the true objective of the legislation. Contrary to the rhetoric, it was not to provide better health care. Given the NSA is capturing data from individuals, and the Internet search engines provide data to political campaigns, data abuse is already pervasive, but barely scratches the surface of the consequences of a national database, where all these data are integrated.

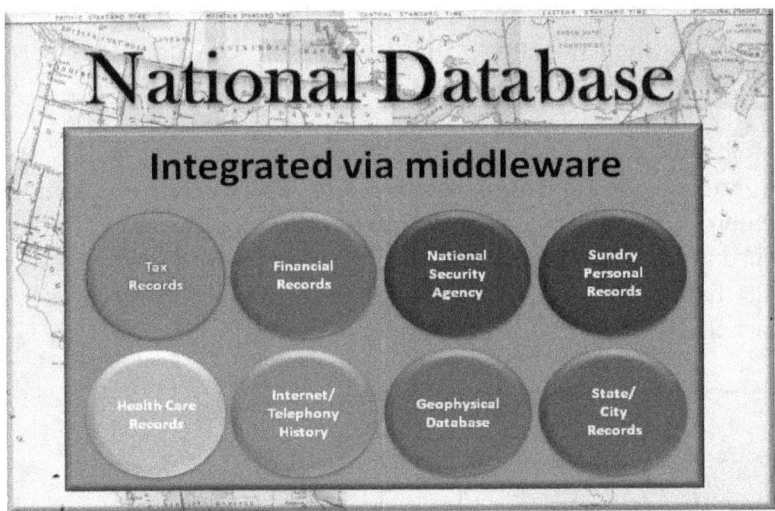

At this point, the distinction between governance and politics becomes vitally important. The definitions from Merriam-Webster serve the purpose.

Politics

"Activities that relate to influencing the actions and policies of a government or getting and keeping power in a government".

Government

"The act or process of governing; *specifically*: authoritative direction or control".

How information is used

Government and business use information for a variety of commercial and private purposes, for and against citizens/consumers. For this paper, there are two major areas of concern. First, the security of our information is a personal and financial issue, covered earlier. The second issue is the overall threat for the media to control and manipulate information to sell us a point of view. Worse, the media can/does cooperate with government to deliver political messages precisely to the consumer. These situations can quickly evolve into "propaganda" and "programming" to control what we do.

The following chart breaks information use into four categories, starting with knowledge, and progressing into social control. Somewhere between propaganda and control, the free press disappears, compromising all personal freedoms and rights. The process can be so subtle that society in general may not realize it has occurred until it is a fait accompli.

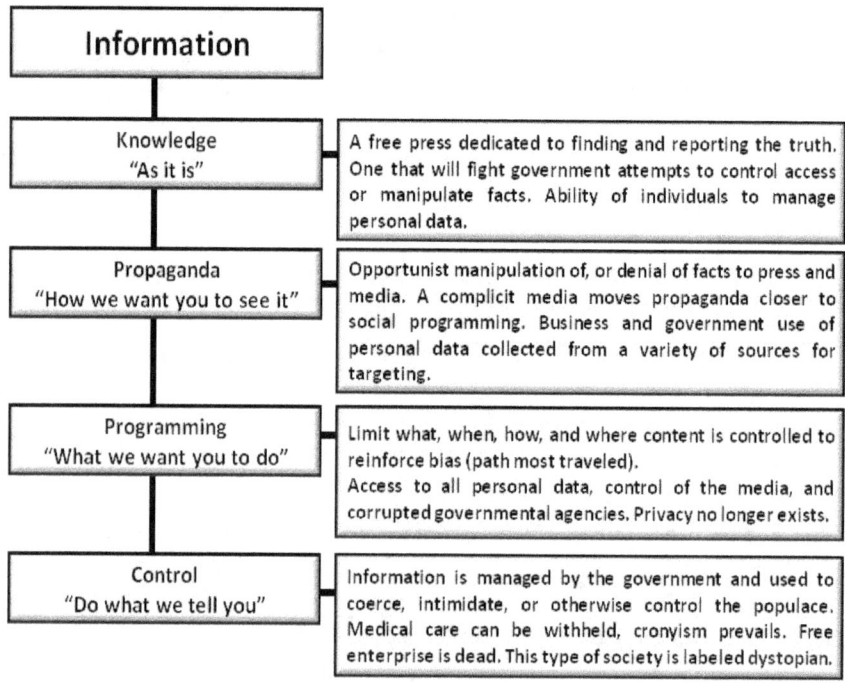

Information	
Knowledge "As it is"	A free press dedicated to finding and reporting the truth. One that will fight government attempts to control access or manipulate facts. Ability of individuals to manage personal data.
Propaganda "How we want you to see it"	Opportunist manipulation of, or denial of facts to press and media. A complicit media moves propaganda closer to social programming. Business and government use of personal data collected from a variety of sources for targeting.
Programming "What we want you to do"	Limit what, when, how, and where content is controlled to reinforce bias (path most traveled). Access to all personal data, control of the media, and corrupted governmental agencies. Privacy no longer exists.
Control "Do what we tell you"	Information is managed by the government and used to coerce, intimidate, or otherwise control the populace. Medical care can be withheld, cronyism prevails. Free enterprise is dead. This type of society is labeled dystopian.

In his book, Nineteen Eighty-Four, George Orwell described a dystopian world called Oceania, where the government controlled everything through the collection and manipulation of information. Our health care records are being integrated with IRS, already proven a great political partner, and not a governmental entity working for the good of the people or the fair application of the law. The national database of you (and me) appears to be an unstoppable reality. The only remaining fight is who will use it and how, and the manner in which we react.

What we can do

There are steps we can take to guard against propaganda and programming. Unfortunately, if we allow ourselves to fall through to the last block, control, the only options are obedience or revolution.

We gather information in small chunks, and it is important to question the validity of every input.

Be aware that we are all biased, and by nature tend to consume information reinforcing those opinions. Try to expand the input base and question the relationships of information.

We rely on expert and group opinion. These sources may be wrong, or manipulated into a course of action.

Be constantly on guard when told to do something for the "greater good." Who established what it means and why should it drive our actions?

From a macro perspective, we need to vote for candidates that actually represent our best interests, and hold them accountable. The freedoms of future generations depend on what we do today.

Epilogue

The Election

The election itself has not affected progress towards building this National database. The resources are under the control of the executive office, and only Congress can prevent the completion of this project.

The Press

The press is a pervasive thread running through the Focused Fire Newsletters. The media stands out as the greatest disappointment relative to the direction in which America is heading. While the actions of President Obama are destructive, the abdication of the press to the political process has long-term consequences to America's liberty.

The Framers carved out a special place for a free press, with the intent that it would stand for the people against governmental abuse. Instead, the press has supported the president on virtually every issue, becoming complicit with the government itself.

The press has not forced accountability on any controversy, including Fast and Furious, Benghazi, the IRS targeting of conservations, or NSA data gathering. The press never made the effort to uncover Obama's past, including birth certificate, college records, thesis, or qualifications for the most important job in the world.

To be fair, the press may be the victim of coercion and bullying, but the interbreeding with government is significant. There are marriages and other personal relationships between governmental officials and the press. For example, David Rhodes, CBS News President, is the brother to Ben Rhodes, an Obama adviser. On Halloween, instead of the press meeting with Josh Earnest, (given the day off), President Obama gave a death by chocolate cake. The cancellation allowed the administration to avoid discussing a significant remark made by Ben Rhodes, referencing the Presidents attempt to bypass Congress on a nuclear arms agreement with Iran.

> "Bottom line is, this is the best opportunity we've had to resolve the Iranian issue diplomatically, certainly since President Obama came to office, and probably since the beginning of the Iraq war," Rhodes said. "So no small opportunity, it's a big deal. This is probably the biggest thing President Obama will do in his second term on foreign policy. This is healthcare for us, just to put it in context."

110

Source: "Obama adviser likened Iran nuclear deal to ObamaCare," By Matthew Continetti, Published October 31, 2014, Washington Free Beacon

Recently, there has been a pushback, as the Obama administration increasingly limits and steps on the press.

A renowned investigative reporter, Sharyl Attkisson, who once worked for CBS, has published her memoir, titled <u>Stonewalled: My Fight for Truth Against the Forces of Obstruction, Intimidation, and Harassment in Obama's Washington.</u>

Other media personalities are speaking out about the lack of transparency and manipulation of the press.

Susan Page, the USA Washington Bureau Chief, stated:

"My big fear is that this administration has been more restrictive and more challenging to the press, more dangerous to the press, really, than any administration in American history in terms of legal investigations and so on. And I think access to the White House has just gotten worse and worse."

http://newsbusters.org/blogs/melissa-mullins/2014/10/31/usa-todays-susan-page-obama-team-most-dangerous-press-us-history#sthash.aViAStJK.dpuf

It is difficult to feel sorry for the press. While they complain, it will not change their behavior. The press prints what the White House provides and ignores the important and controversial issues at the heart of honest governance.

The concerns over the integrity of information have intensified since the publication of this newsletter. There are no guardians at the door.

China

China continually hacks into every American system. China unveiled the Shenyang J-31 Falcon Eagle, a direct clone of the U.S. Joint Strike Fighter, while President Obama was visiting China. America spent billions of dollars developing the fifth-generation fighter, but the Chinese can market theirs as a low-cost alternative, in competition against U.S. manufacturers. Our government will remain silent.

If the Chinese can hack into every other database, why not the National database of you and me? Perhaps North Korea beat them to it.

Industry and consumers alike have become accustomed to hacking attacks. The litany involves Heartland Payment Systems, TJX Companies Inc., Epsilon, Department of Veterans Affairs, Sony PlayStation Network, ESTsoft, AOL, Target and the list goes on. The accumulative effect is millions of personal records potentially hacked with immeasurable consequences, but certainly amounting to hundreds of billions of dollars.

Unfortunately, the attacks have been taking a turn to the darker side. In 2009, the Chinese government attacked Google, Yahoo and other Internet companies. The government gathered data on Chinese human rights leaders, and appropriated intellectual property.

Coercion at a personal level is the new and the most insidious form.

Sony

Sony Entertainment produced a comedy titled "The Interview," starring James Franco and Seth Rogen. Scheduled for release on Christmas day, the plot is an assassination attempt against Kim Jong Un, the supreme leader of North Korea. From all appearances, the Koreans fail to find the film humorous. They reportedly launched a cyber attack against Sony, which included the following e-mail from a group called the "Guardian of Peace," or GOP.

112

"I am the head of GOP who made you worry.

Removing Sony Pictures on earth is a very tiny work for our group which is a worldwide organization. And what we have done so far is only a small part of our further plan. It's your false if you think this crisis will be over after some time. All hope will leave you and Sony Pictures will collapse. This situation is only due to Sony Pictures. Sony Pictures is responsible for whatever the result is. Sony Pictures clings to what is good to nobody from the beginning. It's silly to expect in Sony Pictures to take off us. Sony Pictures makes only useless efforts. One beside you can be our member.

Many things beyond imagination will happen at many places of the world. Our agents find themselves act in necessary places. Please sign your name to object the false of the company at the email address below if you don't want to suffer damage. If you don't, not only you but your family will be in danger.

Nobody can prevent us, but the only way is to follow our demand. If you want to prevent us, make your company behave wisely."

http://variety.com/2014/film/news/hackers-threaten-sony-employees-in-new-email-your-family-will-be-in-danger-1201372230/

Readers need to view this as a dark omen for the future, when the personal National database is complete, everyone can be controlled and manipulated through coercion, reward, and punishment if/when-governmental agencies exploit our information.

This database was and still is the objective of the ACA. To think otherwise is delusional. The only way to stop its completion is to repeal the ACA and disband the IRS by implementing a simplified tax formula.

THE REDISTRIBUTION OF AMERICA

October, 2014 Issue 17

"The <u>power</u> of population is indefinitely greater than the <u>power</u> in the <u>earth</u> to produce subsistence for man" - Thomas Robert <u>Malthus</u>.

Population vs. Resources

Malthus' book fueled a debate that rages to this date. Is the world running out of food and other resources because of population growth?

The three featured works that are foundational to the environmental movement are <u>An Essay on the Principle of Population</u>, <u>The Limits to Growth – A Report for the Club of Rome's Project on the Predicament of Mankind</u>, and <u>Silent Spring</u>.

These first two documents address the relationships and consequences of the dependent relationships between natural and human systems.

An Essay on the Principle of Population, by Malthus, published in 1798, established the framework of dependency between population and resources.

Malthus performed an evaluation of future resource availability based on then known reserves, consumption, circumstances, and population growth. Essentially, he wanted to know how long resources would last given the rate of consumption per human being and the availability of resources (capital). The Limits to Growth expanded the logic.

For Malthus, the relationship between population growth (independent component) and resource limits (dependent) drove the investigation and essay. It is Malthus' contention, and one adopted by subsequent studies, that population growth is exponential, that is "2,4,8,16," while the rate of increased resource availability, or production, is linear, or "1,2,3,4."

The consequences are obvious. That is, consumption will eventually exceed finite production and resources will run out. The following example illustrates both method and logic.

If each person consumes an average of two pounds of food per day, one billion people require two billion pounds of food. This calculation is linear but food consumption is not (linear vs. exponential). Those in the developed countries overindulge as half the world searches for food.

Capital plays a role. Those with wealth or access to capital will hoard the resources, taking a proportionately greater share to distribute among a more affluent, elite population while dividing the smaller portion among the larger, less wealthy population. This effect is obvious in America today as investors gain from an expanding stock market while the middle and less affluent classes lose income and purchasing power.

As the growth rate of the undeveloped countries increases, the consumption of food per individual may stay the same but the total consumption of food increases in direct relationship to the population. As undeveloped countries increase their standard of living and approach the consumption level of the industrialized world, food requirements will multiply due to the increased demand. Eventually, demand may

Self-actualization Personal growth fulfillment Consumption decreases may occur			
Esteem Needs Personal and work achievement, status, responsibility, reputation Larger dwellings, cars, travel options, greater consumption			
Belonging and love needs Family, affection, relationships, work groups, cities, national identity Family, housing, travel, education, consumptive, automation			
Safety needs Shelter, Security, social order, laws, parameters, stability, medical Tribal, more advanced tools			
Biological and Physiological Needs Survival needs – air, food, drink, shelter, warmth, sex, sleep Basic tools			

Greater resource usage (left axis) — *Greater Impact on Ecosystems* (right axis)

Based on Maslow's Hierarchy of Needs
(original five-stage model)

outstrip supply.

The availability of resources is a function of scarcity and price. Those in the developed world, with greater access to capital, will maintain consumption levels at the expense of those financially troubled countries. In this way, capital helps to restore equilibrium and balance between supply and demand. It does not restore parity of access to resources. Supply will control the population as it does in many other animal species, and given a shortage of food, people will die of starvation. The effect is a reduction of population to sustainable levels.

While criticized in some quarters, the methods used by Malthus were valid. The flaws were the same ones encountered by many models, past and present. These are the availability of irrefutable, accurate, detailed information on specific resources and the ability to quantify the potential, timing, and effects of technology.

Unlike Malthus, we have computers that can recalculate every variable in seconds. Without proper data on each variable, however, conclusions calculated in nano-seconds still generate contentious conclusions. The model Malthus employed passed the logic of reasonableness.

The purpose behind Malthus' study is questionable, given that he was an elitist living in England when the slave trade was at its peak, and black and poor people had lower value in that society. His concern was the rapid growth rate of the working class/low-income groups with an accompanying increase in resource competition. It was the beginning of the industrial age. Eli Whitney had developed the cotton gin only five years prior, and the steamboat was a future event. Malthus wanted to determine if there would be enough resources to perpetuate the high standard of living enjoyed by the elite of the day and if not he advocated war, pestilence and other population control devices.

The Limits to Growth, the second, and for our purposes, more significant of the two studies on population and resources was written in 1972 by MIT Project Team authors Donella H. Meadows, Dennis L. Meadows, Jorgen Randers, and William W. Behrens III, and sponsored by The Club of Rome.

While there were numerous studies by a wide range of authors discussing the dependent population/resource relationship, such as in the book Peak Oil, any serious study on the topic referenced or led to The Limits to Growth as the source document. It established a paradigm of intellectual thought and was foundational to the environmental movement. Its concepts are pervasive in the world's culture but often operate in the background or as a part of other social philosophies.

The Limits to Growth struck the chords of a world sick of the Vietnam War and reeling from the freedom movement in the sixties. America was primed for a world cause. China had yet to start its journey into the industrialized world. Computers were still novelties in the workplace.

117

<u>The Limits to Growth</u> study contained research into five specific areas, per the Table of Contents:

- The Nature of Exponential Growth
- The Limits of Exponential Growth
- Growth in the World System
- Technology and the Limits of Growth
- The State of Global Equilibrium

There is not a specific chapter devoted to the topic of the environment, but the environment forms a pervasive thread throughout the work.

The book takes the concepts introduced by Malthus and expands them in relationship to population, finite resources, and sophistication of analytics. The analysts created an early computer model, a fact criticized by those unfamiliar with the power of either modeling or computers. The systems approach was classic and the scientific method impeccably observed. A valid model was carefully constructed, and dependencies, calculations, inputs, outputs, assumptions, and conclusions, clearly documented.

The most significant focal point was over-reach, consuming resources at a rate greater than replenishment, or replaced by substitutes. The question, were resources sustainable at a predictable rate? Using weighting factors significantly changed the resulting calculation but the projected consequence is a function of time, not probability.

The study is sobering. It leaves little doubt that if population grows without restriction, whether resource usage is linear or exponential, we will run out of limited resources in less than one hundred years.

Expanding populations in the developing countries translates into more people attempting to climb the ladder of Maslow's Hierarchy of Needs. Economic expansion accelerated as China and other emerging markets became more industrialized. According to scientists, the exponential consumption of resources is a reality.

Pollution

The Limits to Growth addresses pollution of the biosphere in strong terms. To project the effects of pollution, the authors assigned dependent values to the causes of pollution. This enabled calculations of the projected environmental effects based on resource use and population. They state, "We have almost no knowledge about where the upper limits to these pollution curves might be," meaning they lacked specific knowledge of the effect of resources on the climate, and therefore, the calculated results were relative, not absolute.

While the authors acknowledged shortfalls in data detail, many readers ignored the caveat of "the best available" and used the report and formulas to support conclusions of their own (then and now).

Study Recommendations

One key point was that countries should shift from industrial activity to service and health care sectors, thereby avoiding pollution from production. This had profound and far-reaching effects.

Many entities, including business and government, were excited about this new direction, ignoring the recommendation that America downsize (my word, not theirs) until it reached economic parity with the rest of the world. Business, on the lookout for cheaper production sources, dismantled vertical factories, which performed all the work from foundry through assembly, for core competency, farming out operations to companies that performed them at a lower cost. This horizontal factory system eventually made it easier to offshore operations.

A clean environment became one of society's primary priorities, rightly so given disasters like Love Canal, an industrial chemical waste site. The passage of harsh environmental regulations gave industry the incentive to relocate manufacturing to Mexico, and pollute with impunity, then to China and other developing nations. Manufacturing jobs in America dropped from twenty-five percent of the work force to twelve.

The emergence of the projected solution, an intellectually driven service state, failed to materialize. All global boundaries disappeared with the internet, allowing instant transmission of information and intellectual property across the globe. Technology, the most underestimated component in the studies, destroyed the dream of a giant, vibrant super-service economy before it even left the incubator.

The Limits to Growth provides important insights and relationships into key environmental and social issues. On page 93, the authors disavow any intent at prediction:

> "These graphs are not exact predictions of the value of the variables at any particular year in the future. They are indications of the system's behavioral tendencies only."

While the stated intent was not to make predictions, the methodology itself forces conclusions. All forecasts and predictions are wrong to some degree. Decisions based on data of this type are only as precise as the data, selection of formulas and the methodology.

The authors make a series of recommendations aimed at eco-equilibrium. These include steps to maintain population, resources, and production (capital) in equilibrium, sustaining environmental integrity and conserving resources. The objective was to define methods to delay the effects to the "limits to growth" identified in the study.

These recommendations contain a series of rules governing all human activity. While the book does not specifically recommend a world government, it would be impossible to achieve the objectives without a utopian perspective and a benign authoritarian global government.

Preceding this recommendation, the authors questioned the ability of government to deal with the complexities and variables indicated by the model. It has been my experience that government manages resources poorly. Two quick examples are the U.S. Postal Service and the Veterans Health Care system.

The study proposes the following found on page 171 in <u>The Limits to Growth</u>:

"The capital plant and the population are constant in size."

The birth rate equals the death rate and the capital investment rate equals the depreciation rate.

Based on this recommendation, control of population, the highest priority, means reducing birthrates to correspond to death rates or increasing death rates to match birth rates. Freezing population levels below capital growth and resource usage achieves equilibrium.

One of the tenets is abortion and birth control. While not specifically mentioned, euthanasia is another tool for population control. Part of the phrasing "elimination of unwanted children" provides an answer. If birth control, abstinence, and a higher death rate achieve zero population growth, fewer abortions are required. The reality is that zero growth is difficult to achieve without abortions, a lot of them and euthanasia, a lot of it. The problem is that abortion and euthanasia are murder, and a highly divisive social issue.

The best tool for controlling population is through the health care system. Not coincidentally, the first agenda item for the Obama administration was the Affordable Health Care Act. Coupling the ACA to the Department of Revenue establishes a <u>National Database of You and Me</u>, (see the September Focused Fire Newsletter).

In time, the government will have the capacity, if not the moral authority or support of the people, to ration healthcare as a tool to control population. Obviously, this means the American populace, not the world in general, will pay the price for population control, making more room for immigrants into the United States.

Equally important is a zero growth economy, which allows central control and prevents the over-reach of resource utilization. The authors identify the United States as one country whose standard of living requires a reduction to achieve and maintain global equilibrium.

> "We unequivocally support the contention that a brake imposed on demographic and economic spirals must not lead to a freezing of the status quo of economic development of the world's nations. (Pg. 198). If such a proposal were advanced by the rich nations, it would be taken as a final act of neocolonialism. The achievement of a harmonious state of global economic, social, and ecological equilibrium must be a joint venture based on joint conviction, with benefits for all. The greatest leadership will be demanded from the economically developed countries, for the first step towards such a goal would be for them to encourage deceleration in the growth of their own material output while, at the same time, assisting the developing nations in their efforts to advance their economies more rapidly". <u>The Limits to Growth</u>

Over-reach is not preventable unless every country buys off and complies with the agreement. Taking actions unilaterally, as Obama has in America, will not achieve global equilibrium. It will only destroy America. Who in America specifically voted to downsize our economy and give away our future? By definition, preventing over-reach has a profound effect on economies, commodities, consumerism, travel, and recreation, with freedoms replaced by dystopia.

> "All input and output rates – births, deaths, investment, and depreciation-are kept to a minimum."

This requires strict governmental control preferably at a global level. On one hand it supports the rights of choice but on the other takes them away. China provides a hard example, when the government encouraged rapid population growth, then attempted to limit the consequences by imposing a "one child per family" rule.

> "The levels of capital and population and the ratio of the two are set in accordance with the values of society."

Managing capital and population in accordance with the values of society allows the government tight control over the means of production, pollution, land use, energy usage, and any activity that would upset the environmental equilibrium. The question is who establishes the values? (See the chapter on "Trust.")

Compliance with the recommendations could default into tyranny, resolving one problem but creating a worse one. Is dystopian life worth living? Does it save our species while destroying our humanity?

Theories for reducing population emerged as environmentalists adopted the concepts of the report. The mantra became "zero population growth," with abortion, birth control, and sex education as the primary weapons. The industrialized countries cut birthrates but the emerging countries did not, opening the way for large migrations of legal and illegal immigrants from the poor countries into the industrialized ones. The consequences are still in ongoing, and most are proving to be detrimental to free societies.

There were two sequels to The Limits to Growth. The latest is Limits to Growth, The 40 Year Update.

The Limits to Growth proved to be accurate in many ways based on given scientific data. The most noteworthy issues were global warming and over-reach. There is every reason to believe that over-reach has been significant and will probably increase in the future unless factors slow it down.

The conclusion remains that current levels of consumption and production are not sustainable, and that the world will experience resource shortages. The last report, none-the-less, is optimistic if we are wise enough to take the appropriate actions.

Conclusion

The problem is that discredited and inaccurate data on global warming and population raise questions about the contents of the work.

Surprisingly, much of the rhetoric about the environment is immaterial. Instead of talking about it, we need to take real actions to be environmental stewards.

The word "finite" means "limited" but it does not imply knowledge of what those limitations are. The limits are very complicated to quantify in highly complex systems given the high numbers of variables. Given incomplete data, calculating precise conclusions is difficult. To the credit of the authors of The Limits to Growth, they make this point clear and their generalized conclusions are proving correct. We know, for example, that eventually consumption will reach and exceed capacity. Resources will run out unevenly and one or more essential resources will influence the rates of production or use of other resources. We do not know if technology will have the capability to develop alternate materials, nor solve the problems with pollution.

It is difficult to calculate the rate of discoveries in innovation and technology, given numerous unquantifiable variables. In 1965 Intel cofounder Gordon Moore stated, "The number of transistors incorporated in a chip will approximately double every 24 months." This was labeled "Moore's Law." The computer chip changed everything, moving computer technology, and perhaps other applied sciences, from linear to exponential growth.

Convergence

President Barack Obama was born on August 4, 1961, and was a student in high school and college when the great American outsourcing of jobs began. By then, the universities fully embraced the environmental movement. We know little of his background relative to environmentalism but as a Senator and President, he aligned with the extreme elements of the movement.

In Obama's book, The Audacity of Hope: Thoughts on Reclaiming the American Dream, he makes his opinion clear. America is guilty of neo-colonialism, and much of our wealth was ill earned on the backs of slaves and the developing nations. His presidency has been a work-in-

124

progress to rectify all of these injustices. Given the Law of Unintended Consequences, he created additional layers of injustice against the American people in the process.

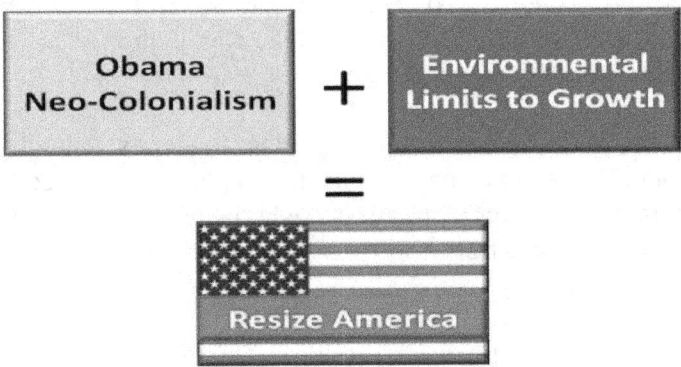

Throughout history, disparate ideals converge, retaining their respective paradigms, but creating intense energy for change. Environmentalism and Obama are uneasy partners in a net sum game where the total resource consumption and capital must remain in equilibrium to achieve sustainability. While environmentalism is concerned about the overall concept of resource conservancy, Obama is committed to an ideology obsessed with how wealth and resources are distributed, who gets what, and who participates in the rewards.

Redistribution means to "divide something among a group in a different way." (Merriam-Webster.) The word gained attention in 2008 when Barack Obama, as a candidate for President of the United States, inadvertently used the term during a discussion with Joe the Plumber.

There was an immediate uproar. The candidate was proposing a socialist concept, the Robin Hood syndrome, where one robs the rich and gives to the poor. It was hyperbole, distracting from an intelligent search for the meaning of the word, and preventing discovery of the consequences behind the word. Had voters spent less time reacting and more time analyzing, they might have discovered what Obama meant when he promised to "fundamentally change America," and realized that it meant the redistribution and downsizing of America.

Examples of redistribution occur everywhere. Parents paying for college, and contributions to church and other charitable donations are redistribution of wealth. Everyone agrees this is proper because it is entirely a matter of personal choice.

Government is involved in redistributing revenues gained through taxation and fees and paying for collective services demanded by law or the population. The problem occurs when government redistributes without authorization from the constituency or for purposes of which we do not approve.

Redistribution as practiced by President Obama is a net sum game where total available resources never change, only which people have access to those resources and therefore gains wealth and power.

If the entire world is involved in a net sum game, global resource utilization remains the same, but both consumption and production move from one location to another. Wealth and power move in relationship, often gradually. China practices growth concepts, and is gaining economic strength and power at our expense.

The traditional American concept of redistribution is equality, which requires taking more from the rich to make sure other people have shelter, food, clothing, health care, and educational opportunities.

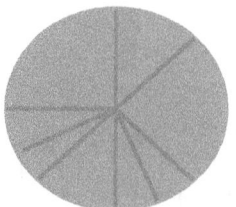 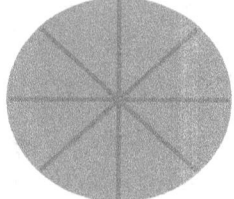

This concept extends to other humanitarian activities when we want to use some of our resources to help others in the global community. This raises a difficult question. How much is a "fair share" and how high is the price society must pay to help others throughout the world? What costs will be incurred at the expense of our current economy? How will this attempt at parity affect those citizens trapped by a changing workplace? What happens to the future prospects of our younger generations?

Obama's concept of redistribution extends far beyond the rich sharing more with the poor. His vision is vastly different, redistributing wealth to the third world while downsizing America in the world economy and as a super-power.

While one could say that he has never stated this purpose, the results of his actions make the objective very clear. Much of what he wanted to accomplish is completed. We are a weaker country and our economy has deteriorated. The question is whether he understood the consequences of these objectives on America and the world. Even more troubling, do the citizens of America comprehend the multitude of ways the completion of <u>Obama's</u> dream changed the way we live and the world our children and grandchildren will inherit? Given a license to continue with his agenda for another two years, are the consequences irrevocable?

Consequences

Money moves globally and capital will grow somewhere regardless of how much is redistributed. Our national debt is nearly $18 trillion dollars, while our annual GDP is $16 trillion (http://www.multpl.com/us-gdp-inflation-adjusted/table). Eventually, this debt must be repaid, and our economy will be redistributed and diluted.

The two most significant policies leading to equilibrium are population and controlling the means of production and distribution. The solution itself calls for a radical reduction in manufacturing, which drives wealth creation. Cutting production, in turn, reduces economic strength and the ability to deal with environmental issues.

In extreme environmentalism, both production and consumption shrink to fit the capability of the planet to provide resources (equilibrium) while retaining sustainability. In this case, the net sum game is not applicable because environmentalism demands a significant reduction in the size of the pie, or the total resources used. Given this scenario, there will be winners and a greater number of losers. The United States has and will continue to suffer substantial wealth degeneration, and an inability to create jobs. We have high debt with inadequate investment and incentive to sustain the nation's wealth.

As our economy falters or is permanently weakened, the environmental standards will collapse. Rich nations can afford environmental laws, but the environment suffers when wealth formation is restricted. In a controlled, dystopian society, resources and wealth migrate to the elite and everyone else gets the leftovers. If nothing is left, nature serves to constrain distribution. Given the massive redistribution currently in progress in the United States, we will unilaterally reduce our standards to the level of more restrictive nations. By allowing ourselves to enter a state of economic freefall, we risk becoming a third world country.

http://competitiveamerica.us/ we make the following observation.

This Cairo, Egypt resident dumps garbage next to a container.

Ships shrouded by smog in China.

When economies collapse, the net sum game is operational, and necessity trumps basic environmental preservation. Americans foolishly believe it could never happen here.

Look around at the empty factories. Drive through the inner cities (like that of Detroit). Serve at a food kitchen and see how people live without jobs. Afterward, listen to the rhetoric about how things are getting better. Think about political correctness. Consider the constant reshaping and programming that result from a corrupted political process, press and education systems.

Ask why our factory jobs have fled the country. Ask why the greatest country ever on this planet is unable to generate jobs, educate its people, preserve its environment, and lead the way to a higher human state.

Study the history of Argentina.

Solutions

America needs a free enterprise system that distributes wealth and opportunity by investment and capability. Consumer demand determines winners and losers, rewarding cost-effective products manufactured in environmentally friendly facilities. Customers (we the people) establish the true value by our interaction with the marketplace. The problem is that customers, even many environmentalists, buy the lowest-cost imports without considering the source. Did production occur in sweatshops using child labor, with waste dumped into the air and water? Did we reward bad behavior? The hypocrisy is the passage of laws that drive jobs overseas, preaching a clean environment, and buying a product from offshore facilities. Perhaps environmentalism translates to "not in my backyard." The kinds of pollution creating the greatest environmental damage are global, and "out of sight, out of mind" is delusional.

There are Americans who have lost faith that God has blessed our country. Just as the world reached theoretical peak oil production, and we were about to suffer enormous increases in energy prices, a technological miracle occurred in the discovery of greater than one hundred year's supply of natural gas. This discovery, and the wealth and influence it generates, will be the foundation for our economic recovery after Obama leaves office. Free enterprise, science, and education must use technology as a bridge opportunity for the development of environmentally friendly energy sources. The world may not get another chance and independence from hydrocarbons must remain an international objective. God gave us time. Saved from redistribution and downsizing, let us not waste our opportunity.

Solutions must prevent environmental degradation

Free enterprise cannot allow greed for money and power to govern who we are as people. Manufacturing must build environmentally friendly facilities and products. The populace must learn if they want a clean environment to buy from green factories, even if paying more. Buying from American sources takes thousands of polluting cargo ships off the world's waterways.

Given the large supplies of natural gas, significant transportation sectors could switch energy sources, reducing greenhouse gases and setting America free from the Middle East. This has the effect of taking thousands of polluting oil tankers off the earth's waterways, and reduces our risks of continually meddling in the Middle East, where they love our money but hate the freedoms we stand for.

Voting against the Obama agenda does not mean setting back the environmental clock; it actually means moving it forward. When America is strong and independent and its entrepreneurial spirit free to develop we will once again pursue the rewards of the great American experiment. We can and must preserve those wilderness areas where our spirits can reach up and touch God's fingertips, and leave a legacy of clean air and water to the future generations of the world.

Thank you, God.

General Sherman
Sequoia National Park, California

Epilogue

Downsizing

Outsourcing jobs began with the Carter administration and leveled out under Presidents Reagan, G. H. W. Bush, and Clinton. The second outsourcing of jobs from America began in 2001, under George W. Bush, losing nearly seven million jobs, and continues under Barack Obama. (Source: Bloomberg Government). In 2013 alone, 2,637,239 jobs were outsourced. (Source: Sourcing Line Computer Economics).

Consequences

The industrialized civilizations are working hard to save our environment. The Western civilizations, Europe, Canada, and the United States, have practiced the principle of zero population growth, and severely reduced greenhouse gasses. While feel good achievements, we have launched potential long-term consequences.

Environment

Most of the world, including China, has lesser concerns for the environment, trading it for economic advantage, or they are unable to invest in the technologies and clean-up efforts.

This year, China surged past the United States in industrial output. The following chart shows Green House Gas (GHG) emissions and industrial output in relation to country and equivalent pollution ratios.

	China	USA
GHG Emissions	9679.30	6668.79
Ind. Output (Trillion$)	2.9	2.43
Ind. OP % USA +China	54.4	45.6
GHG % USA+China	59.2	40.8
Ratio	1.17	.89

The last line shows the ratio of pollution percentages vs. manufacturing output in total between the two countries. The ratio of GHG emissions per volume is much lower for the United States than for China.

As a country, we passed our industrial pollution to China and other producing countries, along with jobs, then buy their goods, punishing our more environmentally friendly factory system. Of great concern is the profound hypocrisy of environmentalism, constantly pushing for tighter controls in America, while remaining quiet about international polluters. Where is the global outrage? Where is the protest from American environmentalists? Why are we downsizing America to the benefit of our economic competitors? *This is madness.*

Population

Western civilization adopted the principles of extreme environmentalism to control population. The balance of the world did not. This created a void, and immigrants from third-world countries who do not share Western values, flooded into the space. Eventually, those populations may become the majority.

In the final analysis, we are not actually saving the environment, but destroying America, as we know it. Western civilization may be changing its value systems in response to demographic turnover and perhaps on the path to self-destruction. The good news is that once we are aware of the issues, positive actions can change the course of destiny.

YOUR CHOICE - POLICY OR OPPORTUNITY DRIVEN SOCIETY

November, 2014 Issue 18

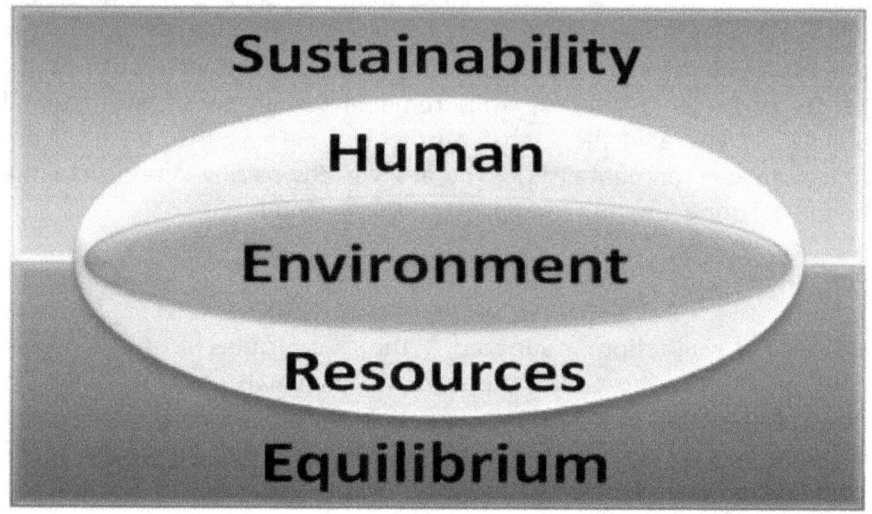

Life in a Policy Driven Society
Basic forms of governance
Sustainability
Human
Environment
Resources
Equilibrium
Opportunity

Life in a Policy Driven Society

For the past six years, Americans have experienced life in a policy driven, dependency economy where the government exercises ever-tighter constraints while dodging responsibility and discouraging transparency. Labeled "the new normal," the myth of "for the greater good" perpetuates this economic malaise.

America voted twice for this economic model. In 2008, they voted in the Democratic Party, led by President Barack Obama. In 2012, in spite of a poorly performing economy and dishonest governance, they voted to renew his efforts. The Redistribution of America, last month's Focused Fire Newsletter, covered this topic.

The net result of the last six years is a country and world that emulates the president. Trust is a rare commodity, and virtually no one believes what President Obama says. This distrust has brought the normal flow of governing to a halt, and slashed American's influence and strength in the global arena.

America needs to rebuild an opportunity society, where hard work and effort pay off for the individual and society in general. An opportunity society is free market based, but differs from capitalism or laissez faire on two important points. First, the concept does not support the exploitation of labor, capital, and resources for pure monetary gain. A clean environment and personal freedoms are prerequisites. Second, it does not reject the regulations required to prevent systemic abuse.

At the same time, in an opportunity society, government cannot exploit business, labor, capital, and resources to achieve unrealistic or artificial economic parity. It is not free to implement transformational programs, by any name, without the consent of the people. Government cannot use its position to justify and/or achieve dystopian objectives. When it attempts to do so, historically, it actually increases the overall waste through the cost of government and the inefficiencies implicit in "big bureaucratic systems," while wreaking lasting damage to our freedoms.

It would be easy to drift into an idealistic discussion, defining unworkable concepts, but from a systems perspective, all ideas and actions must spring from the same thought and effort, with pragmatic application. To achieve these purposes requires a clear and practical description of an "opportunity driven society." First, we must construct some conceptual foundation.

Basic forms of governance

There are two fundamental organizational structures, hierarchal and self-organizing.

The traditional organizational structure is a hierarchy. The upper tier is independent (causal), and all the other layers are dependent (effect). Power is concentrated at the top and distributed by direction and control through the layers within the organization, with the expectation that all will agree and comply with the directive. Failure is interpreted as insubordination and the penalties are sometimes severe.

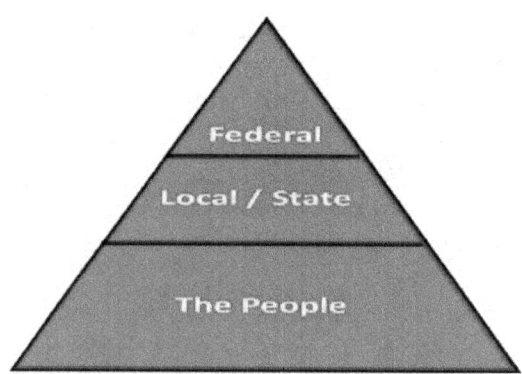

Hierarchal forms of government include dictatorships, monarchies, socialism, and dystopia. In these structures, the term equality and hierarchy are an oxymoron. A hierarchy controls and distributes power and wealth down through a dependent constituency and promotes a greater good, often meaning whatever goals the bureaucracy needs to sustain its power or reach its objectives.

The government determines which freedoms the people can enjoy, with wealth and resources managed directly or through regulatory mechanisms. Bureaucrats choose which laws to enforce, and which legal violations to investigate or tolerate, and the government avoids accountability by manipulating or controlling information. The government has the power over the people, who are accountable to the government. The government rewards those who support its actions, and punishes those that do not.

The tiers within a hierarchy take many forms, but equality is not one of them. Pick up the business section of any newspaper and it is apparent the rich are benefiting from the stock market. The poor are increasingly supported by public assistance, and the middle class is shrinking. It seems obvious, but this type of redistribution and downsizing of America is resulting in a poorer, inequitable economy and society by design of our own federal government.

Complexity occurs because many activities within a hierarchy are not dependent. Persons responsible for achieving the delegated tasks have free thought and independent action. Hierarchies incorrectly assume shared values and purpose. Each level filters directives, and people may not choose to execute them. Sometimes, the metrics failed to hold them accountable, but more frequently they do not see any reason to do it or believe it harmful. People have different agendas, perspectives, and knowledge. Every person makes decisions daily that affect varying degrees of performance.

Self-organizing—the second concept partially originates in complex adaptive theory. In summary, it states that all groups of people develop their own culture, beliefs, and sets of values. They select leaders, and perform work to self-determined standards. Natural work groups are rooted in this concept. Actually, self-organizing groups flourish even within hierarchies. The problem is when they take action contrary to the directions given from the top.

Democracy and Federalism are special examples of self-organizing systems. The people set the policies and elect an abbreviated form of hierarchy to govern. The purpose is the common good, such as protection, administration of laws, and faithful and equal promotion of the best societal interests. In a democracy, the people determine "the greater good," and government helps the people achieve those objectives. Conflicted, Americans are partially operating under both forms of government, and many suffer from political schizophrenia.

It is remarkable, given the opportunity to be king, that George Washington refused, aware that the secret to a successful country was free people. He and the other founders established a miracle of governance that continues until this day. In our form of government, the people have the final say. The people elect the appropriate local and state governments, granting them the primary authority to do the peoples will. That is, pass and enforce laws, build roads and structures, provide education, and in general, provide for the collective needs of the people.

America has a federal government to establish laws over the collection of states. Under the Constitution, it has only the power delegated by the states. The primary mission of centralized government is protecting the citizens and enforcing the freedoms guaranteed by the Constitution. In this structure, the power remains with the people, per the following illustration. In the parallel illustration, freedoms equate to structure. As long as the people have the power, they retain all the freedoms.

These guiding principles are under attack, as our current leaders

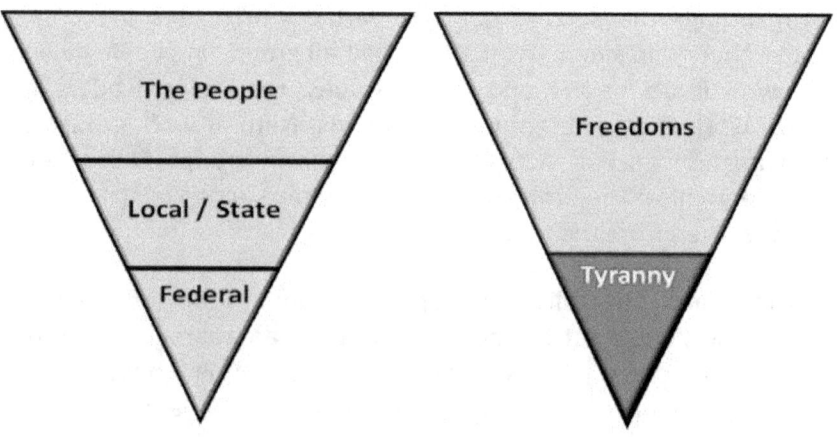

attempt to flip the country from, "<u>we</u> the people," to "<u>me</u> the government." We must not deceive ourselves, both parties are complicit in the effort to divide the people and share the spoils. The difference is that President Obama provides leadership to people that have demonstrated their mission - to change America through the mechanisms of redistribution and downsizing, powered by a policy driven, top-down system. (Read the previous Focused Fire Newsletter for deeper descriptions of these terms).

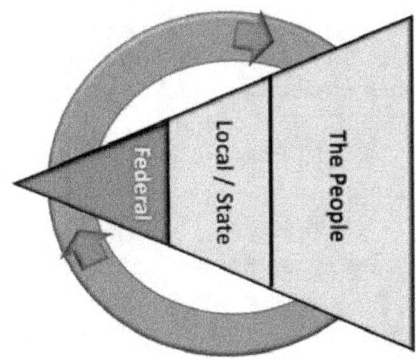

These two perspectives dictate different responses and governing styles. Hierarchical systems are directing while self-organizing systems imply enabling. Hierarchal systems are not democratic, and the power always accumulates at the top. History teaches us lessons, among them the sad truth that forfeited freedoms do not come back.

Given this general foundation, we can get into the specifics of an opportunity driven society.

Merriam-Webster

op·por·tu·ni·ty - an amount of time or a situation in which something can be done
>   1. a favorable juncture of circumstance
>   2. a good chance for advancement or progress

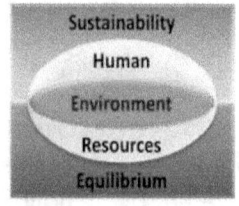

We developed the lead icon to illustrate an opportunity driven society, addressing the principles and tradeoffs of sustainability, human needs, the environment, resources, and equilibrium.

Sustainability

America must sustain itself as a nation. This requires jobs, an exceptional education system, entrepreneurs, invention, and innovation. This also translates into a strong industrial and service sector. Industry not only increases national power, but it is foundational for economic sustainability. For the last six years, government has blamed business for all social ills, and then reached deeply into industry's pockets for political contributions.

We need a strong and committed military to protect our lives, physical world, and our freedoms. When the United States leads, the world does better, but we must not police the world. At the same time, we need to provide leadership or others will do so, specifically China, Russia, and groups like ISIS. The failure to make a decision and take positive action always means living with the default, directions determined by others, and suffer the consequences of their decisions.

We need to hold the press accountable for keeping us accurately informed. Without a free and honest press, democracy will fall. Our manipulated press now serves no purpose beyond propaganda.

Technology has been the perennial scapegoat for destroying the environment. Like money and other fungible (interchangeable) concepts, technology has application for positive or negative purposes. In this case, it will ensure the survival or destruction of the human species. There are a number of presentations on CompetitiveAmerica.us showing high-technology applications in manufacturing and food production. Manufacturing technologies, specifically miniaturization and lean programs, will reduce resource requirements. Food technology, the Green Revolution, saved millions from starving. Without

142

advanced agriculture, many millions are destined to die. Who wants to be the person that tells them, "We want to preserve our environment for the future. I'm sorry, but that means you and your children must starve, for the greater good."

America is the most innovative country in the world and must sustain that comparative advantage. Technology, across all disciplines and fields of study, brings great opportunities for knowledge and convergence, and applied knowledge power's innovation. Enterprises need to think in terms of structures and systems that promote innovation. While partially addressed by the Lean philosophy, the thought process needs to expand and encompass disruptive technologies, and breakthrough products. These will generate situations and risks, convertible into opportunities. American industry, powered by a free society of workers and a national curiosity, will continue to be the world leader in innovation.

American manufacturers are rethinking the factory system in terms of new energy sources, automation, and the environment. The investment in advanced technologies will result in a factory system premised on energy conservation and environmental integrity.

Human

Promote the freedoms guaranteed by the Constitution. We are a nation subject to the equal application of the Rule of Law. Elected officials take an oath to uphold and enforce the laws and are responsible and accountable to the constituents, not the people to government. When they fail at this primary task, throw them out.

Free the people to create and build on entrepreneurial opportunities without excessive intervention or regulation by government, as long as they comply with a fair set of regulations. This is an opportunity driven system with incentives and rewards worth the passion and effort required to make good things happen. This incentive fuels free enterprise, and creates businesses, services, and jobs. Slant the reward system to the producers and entrepreneurs instead of non-productive

143

members of society. Build systems that provide food, shelter, and clothing for those in need.

Admit the numerous shortcomings in the Affordable Care Act. Restructure the health care system to provide comprehensive services at affordable prices. Start by revamping the Tort system.

Encourage entrepreneurship and innovation in education. There has been an accumulative shortage of advanced applied technology workers for ten years, yet the education system is still behind the curve. We know that bureaucracies take time to react; did that contribute to the failure to fill the education gap?

Create a student centric education system that prepares graduates for a realistic future job market. Start by returning the responsibility to the educators at the state level, who are far better prepared to educate the people than federal government bureaucrats. Use education to create equal opportunities regardless of gender, color, or religion.

Take the money spent at the federal level and return it to the states, but use it for education. Increase teachers' salaries to professional levels and make sure every student has the needed materials. Educators should not have to form a union to make an equitable salary, buy teaching materials from personal income, or ask family members to contribute supplies. Use some of the money saved by eliminating the federal bureaucracy to make quantum improvements in the schools located in troubled/poor areas. Until society can find a way to integrate low-opportunity students, equality is a buzzword.

Environment

Reducing the environmental impact of human activity is a social cause. Every enterprise needs to address the environment in the governance process. The most significant issues are finding ways to cost effectively incorporate solutions into products, processes, buildings, and everyday practice.

The Second industrial revolution raped the environment and companies all over the world continue the practice. American industry must be ecologically responsible. It is a given, that environmental controls increase the cost of production, and global competitors save money by dumping industrial waste into the air and water. Consumers must learn to reward ecological stewardship, for example, buy from responsible American manufacturers instead of purchasing products made in polluting factories and/or using child labor.

Resources

The world is a finite sphere of eco-dependencies, filled with limited resources, multiple life forms, and endless possibilities. All systems create resource damage or waste. There are earthquakes, forest fires, and a long list of other natural disasters. Humans dig holes, spread fertilizer, cut forests, and apply chemicals, all creating waste, and environmental destruction. All human systems generate pollution of some type, such as carbon dioxide. Academics argue about the causes for global warming. The realist understands that dumping pollutants into a fixed space will eventually render it unusable, and finite resources of some types will run out.

Limited resources with increased demand create a paradox. How can humans produce and consume without destroying the environment? It appears that we have reached a lose-lose position without resolution. In spite of rhetoric, customers will continue to consume, and industry will provide goods and services. All will contribute to resource waste.

The answers are obvious and pragmatic.

- Take responsibility for resource conservation and replenishment.
- Take actions to increase productivity throughout the eco-dependencies, in the plant, office and at home.
- Recognize the importance of convergence, integrating the business enterprise to increase speed but function in sync.

- Reduce waste by buying from responsible suppliers while practicing cradle to grave recycling.
- Spend money on developing technology to create new, more sustainable materials.
- Build products designed/engineered/manufactured for recycling.
- Recycle "everything"
- Build quality products
- Repurpose where possible
- Adopt a "zero waste" attitude while knowing it is an unreachable objective

We must lead the world in scientific investigation and rapidly deploy technologies to insure clean food and water supplies, worldwide. We can contribute far more to the world with entrepreneurship and technology than by redistributing resources and energy to the point of diminishing return.

"Give a person food and teach a person how to build a fire, and they can be warm and filled until the food and fuel run out.

Teach a person how to make tools, and they will make an ax and cut the wood needed for the fire, a hoe to till the soil, and a hammer to build shelter.

Teach a person how to think, innovate, make decisions, and they can build a fire, make tools, grow food, get energy, and exploit opportunities.

Teach people how to collaborate, and they will combine knowledge, innovate, heal the sick, and break technological barriers."

America has once again become the energy center of the world. Energy cost and availability will affect products, processes, and performance. Customers and suppliers face a new set of opportunities. While there are risks in taking action, the risk of doing nothing is inconceivable. It is a simple task to look at the new energy-related technologies and find that change, and obsolescence will be pervasive as this paradigm shift gains power. The government needs to enable clean energy research, but avoid direct investments that end in disaster, such as Solyndra.

Equilibrium

Equilibrium is balance, implying responsible choices. In a civilized democracy, the people must have trust in what their government does, and confidence in a shared "for the greater good."

Develop a clear, concise direction and focused objectives, followed by a path to achieve them. The process is interactive, using the planning tools found in formal process improvement programs such as Lean.

Find a balance between the governed and the government. This is not Democrats vs. Republicans; it is we the people against the abuse of power by both parties.

Government must live within its means, with a zero national debt.

Finding a way towards balance between population, resources, and the environment will be difficult. Since 1973, the native population of America reached equilibrium with zero growth, by reducing birth rates, and nearly 50 million abortions. Immigration filled the void.

The argument about environmental equilibrium is useless unless the rest of the world joins the issue. It makes little sense to continue to cut the opportunities for the future of American children when we have decided, informally, to reduce our own population, redistribute our wealth, and downsize our global economic and military power. Diluted by unskilled workers, our old pay scale was undercut, a contributing factor to the reduction in take-home pay.

147

Opportunity

America needs leadership, a plan, and resolve to rebuild an opportunity driven economy to replace the net sum, policy-driven one we are in the process of creating. To get there, we must reject two phony premises.

First, the "new normal," a government created condition where citizens expect fewer opportunities, lower pay, and restricted personal growth. The "new normal" is the result of a policy-driven society, and the condition is not predestined or normal.

Second, people say our greatest days are behind us, and while untrue, it may become a self-fulfilling prophecy.

Our government is politically motivated and intrusive, acting in its own best interest instead of doing the will of the people. That means business, education, entrepreneurs, and concerned citizens must work together to change America to an opportunity society. We owe it to our children and grandchildren.

American citizens will go to the polls this November. If the Democrats retain a majority, the situation, as experienced for the last six years, will continue. If the Democrats lose the Senate, the country may reach a constitutional crisis if the President decides to take unilateral actions. President Obama may use pen and telephone to take over America, eliminating your rights to freedoms of religion, speech, and to bear arms, and will still the voice of opposition. If my Democratic friends think this is hyperbole, please tell me, "What evidence do you have that he will respect your freedoms?"

Failure to cast a ballot is the equivalent to a yes for the Obama agenda. We have a personal choice. I will vote just as much against the Obama agenda as for a Republican, then start on the newly elected officials to build an opportunity driven society.

148

THE ZONE OF OPPORTUNITY

The Election Results
What the people want
Presidential Reaction
Response
Restore Power to the People
Interpretation
An Action Agenda

The ESC (escape) button on a computer keyboard allows the user to cancel the current process. On November 4, 2014, the American people hit the political ESC key, voting against the Obama administration agenda.

The Election Results

The election was the result of two forces. One was the incentivized Republicans, and the other a distrust of the president and the rejection of his policies. At the same time, the Republicans, with majorities in both the House and the Senate, need not celebrate. They offered few positive plans to move the country forward.

What the people want

The election was about the concerns of the American people; most believe we are far from agreement on direction. Searching for answers, we analyzed numerous polls. Democrats and Republicans have different priorities, but the top five issues are on both lists. The following Pareto Chart is a summary of those analyzed polls.

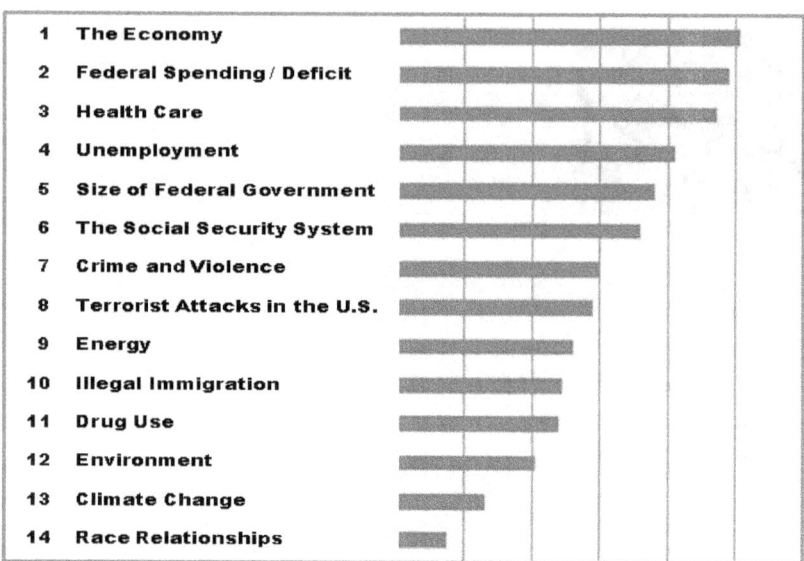

1	The Economy
2	Federal Spending / Deficit
3	Health Care
4	Unemployment
5	Size of Federal Government
6	The Social Security System
7	Crime and Violence
8	Terrorist Attacks in the U.S.
9	Energy
10	Illegal Immigration
11	Drug Use
12	Environment
13	Climate Change
14	Race Relationships

The questions used in the surveys are partially responsible for the answers. None of the major polls included loss of freedoms, cyber crime, or international trade.

One of the polls ranked the problems as:

1 Unemployment
2 Dissatisfaction with government/congress/politicians: poor leadership/corruption/abuse of power
3 Economy
4 Health Care
5 Government debt

http://www.chron.com/news/nation-world/nation/article/Americans

Conspicuously missing from all the lists is global competition. China just passed the U.S. in industrial output, and their continued predatory practices are draining our economy. Their harsh and long-term currency manipulation makes it difficult for American manufacturers to compete. In addition, China steals our intellectual property rights with impunity. Between China and a wasteful government, of both parties, we are $18 trillion dollars in debt, more than one year of our GDP.

Presidential Reaction

The Presidents response to the recent election was to ignore the results, immediately issuing executive orders to implement an immigration program.

While unable to predict the President's actions, as citizens we can extrapolate the future based on demonstrated performance. It is useful to revisit an important period of his development. He was and appears to be a disciple of Saul Alinsky, sharing his method if not his value system.

Following are Alinsky's Rules for Radicals.

1. Power is not only what you have but what the enemy thinks you have.
2. Never go outside the experience of your people.
3. Wherever possible go outside the experience of the enemy. Here you want to cause confusion, fear, and retreat.
4. Make the enemy live up to their own book of rules.
5. Ridicule is man's most potent weapon.
6. A good tactic is one that your people enjoy.
7. A tactic that drags on too long becomes a drag.
8. Keep the pressure on.
9. The threat is usually more terrifying than the thing itself.
10. The major premise for tactics is the development of operations that will maintain a constant pressure upon the opposition.
11. If you push a negative hard and deep enough it will break through into its counter side.
12. The price of a successful attack is a constructive alternative.
13. Pick the target, freeze it, personalize it, and polarize it.
Source: http://townhall.com/columnists/johnhawkins/

151

Obvious by its absence are the rules Americans live by.

- Honesty
- Trustworthiness
- Integrity
- Transparency
- Responsibility
- Hard work
- Concern for others
- Allegiance to God and country
- Freedom of choice
- Freedom of religion
- Fiscal responsibility

Alinsky's Rules for Radicals are a recipe for social manipulation, and sharply contrast with traditional American values. Please note that rule four, "Make the enemy live up to their own book of rules," means to force us to practice our values, but not let us use their rules against them. In other words, take a knife to a gunfight.

We need to consider the consequences of a National database controlled by people in power motivated by Alinsky's Rules for Radicals.

With this understanding, our perspective sharpens on the Presidents priorities, specifically on immigration, which failed to score above tenth place on any poll we researched. Why?

Another past master answers the question.

> "Hence that general is skilful in attack whose opponent does not know what to defend; and he is skilful in defense whose opponent does not know what to attack." Sun Tzu

> http://www.brainyquote.com/quotes/quotes/s/suntzu399627.html#hHIEWUlxFWtebXMW.99

The immigration issue is disruptive, diversionary, and serves President Obama's purpose. While everyone looks at the diversion, he is proceeding without restraints on his primary objective. To use the considerable bureaucracy at his disposal to fundamentally, and obsessively, restructure America. Weakened economically, socially, militarily, and as a global power, he can continue to downsize, redistribute, and dilute America, as long as he has the power to shape policies and actions. He has demonstrated the intent to push the powers of the office to the edge of, and beyond its limits.

The President and Congress can propose legislation but only Congress can make laws. If a President disagrees with the legislation, he/she has the power of veto. Congress and the Senate have the power to override the president's veto, or to withhold funds from the program. Once the legislation is established law, the Presidents job is to enforce it.

President Obama will potentially use executive powers to tighten Environmental Protection Agency (EPA) regulations, and impose other regulatory constraints. He may take highly contentious actions to force his ideals on the country, or to lock the Republicans into non-productive activities, like baiting them to impeach him. In the process, he may over-reach and create a constitutional crisis, if we are not already in one, resulting in investigations, lawsuits, and gridlock.

If the President over-reaches on regulation, international treaties, e.g. gun laws, and deliberately bypasses Congress, events that are truly impeachable violations, the system must appropriately react. The potential consequences are severe, preventing the resolution of greater issues and further endangering the Republic. The country does not need this negativity and cannot afford to waste the next two years through non-productive activities, such as impeachment.

Immersed in divisive social issues of race and political party, and split among ourselves, the focus is on the wrong priorities. We need to fix our economy, strengthen our position in global competition, and grow the economy to provide jobs and opportunities for every American.

China is our enemy. ISIS is our enemy, and poverty is our enemy. Most Americans will agree - my neighbor, regardless of race, religion, political party, gender, or place in society, IS NOT MY ENEMY.

Response

The Framers carefully constructed the balance of government between the executive, legislative, and judicial branches to guard against executive over-reach. They designed the system to respond slowly and deliberately to prevent excessive action and reaction. For that reason, we are not out of danger. Citizens are becoming increasingly aware of the magnitude of the changes, and the potential consequences of redistribution, downsizing, unilateral actions, and presidential over-reach.

States, legislators and businesses have filed lawsuits on immigration and the ACA. The judicial system has been slow to react to an executive over-reach and reluctant to reverse legislation, as witnessed by rulings dealing with the ACA. For that reason, the impact of the courts is uncertain. By the time they act on some of the more critical issues, it may be too late to reverse the course of history.

The Republicans appear to recognize there is nowhere to hide. Harry Reid does not have the authority to block legislation and the Republicans are responsible for legislation. Theoretically, an opportunity exists to pass meaningful laws on energy, immigration, and modifications to the ACA, but the president has veto power. Perhaps the two parties will have the courage to set partisan politics aside and override vetoes on bills that are important to the American people. After all, the source of the problem is leadership.

There will be one year, 2015, where our government has a window to do the peoples work. The potential exists for all branches of government to work together and enable an opportunity driven society. Note, however, that President Obama has never shown an inclination to move in that direction. His actions to date have been the inverse of those needed to recharge America. There will be conflicts between the

Executive and Legislative branches. Based on history, the judicial branch reacts too slowly to play a short-term part in shaping the government, and is perhaps irrelevant as the third party of government. The state governors may represent the greatest power for change.

Our political system faces two years of severe testing, leading up to the presidential election of 2016, when partisan politics once again preoccupy politicians. Nothing useful will occur. The conflicts over policy will be real, numerous, and contentious.

Restore Power to the People

Restore is a computer term that means returning the operating system to an earlier version. The user has the option of picking what version of the past they want to replicate.

The American people are looking for a restore point, and are close to agreement on priorities. It would be uncomplicated if we could duplicate a past period, but time, technology and knowledge change. It is more logical and useful to base a restore point on values instead of a point in time. The greatest value is the power of the American people.

Neither President Obama, nor any American president, is entitled to author and dictate our future without transparency and input from the people. Fraud, like the ACA, is illegal regardless of who perpetrates it. The people must write the story of democracy and make sure it has a successful conclusion.

Our politicians will spend the next two years defining America in terms they understand, but that is inadequate. We may be in the same quagmire, given the contention and gridlock. They will suggest programs to move America ahead, bypassing the important process step of discovering what the citizens want, and developing a national mission spelling out the components of "a greater good."

The following illustration visualizes the concept of an opportunity driven society, as defined in the November newsletter, Issue 18.

The objective is to find the right balance between competing issues. We must be free people, but believe in and practice the rule of law.

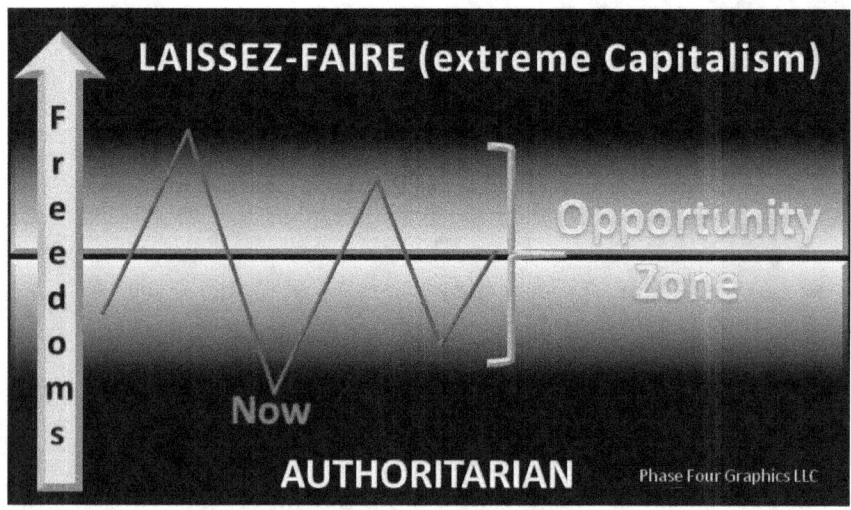

Nearly all quality systems use charts of this type, where parameters (upper and lower control limits) are established. The components of the above chart are:

Lais·sez-faire - https://www.google.com/
    1   A policy or attitude of letting things take their own course, without interfering.

2 Abstention by governments from interfering in the workings of the free market. "laissez-faire capitalism"

Freedom - http://dictionary.reference.com
   1 The state of being <u>free</u> or at liberty rather than in confinement or under physical restraint: *He won his freedom after a retrial.*
   2 Exemption from external control, interference, regulation, etc.
   3 The power to determine action without restraint.
   4 Political or national independence.
   5 Personal liberty, as opposed to bondage or slavery; *a slave who bought his freedom.*
   6 Exemption from the presence of anything specified: *freedom from fear.*
   7 The absence of or release from ties, obligations, etc.

Authoritarian - <u>https://www.google.com/</u>

   1 Favoring or enforcing strict obedience to authority, especially that of the government, at the expense of personal freedom. "the transition from an authoritarian to a democratic regime" <u>autocratic, dictatorial, despotic, tyrannical, draconian, oppressive, repressive, illiberal, undemocratic;</u>
   2 An authoritarian person. <u>Autocrat, despot, dictator, tyrant</u>

Interpretation

The second industrial revolution was a period of extreme laissez-faire, with all the associated negatives.

- Polluted air and water
- Entire areas poisoned with dioxin, PCBs, DDT, and asbestos.
- Labor, including child labor, poorly treated.
- Workplace safety largely ignored.

It was also a period where powerful forces of entrepreneurism built an industrial system that continues to sustain America. The factory system created the American middle class.

157

The opposite of unconstrained capitalism is authoritarianism, where the government manages every means of production and distribution, and controls the actions of the people. Over control and over regulation are both traits of an authoritarian state.

At one extreme, the top of the chart, there are few laws and regulations regarding capital. Everyone has complete freedom to take any action, until someone or something stops it.

On the bottom, authoritarianism, "someone" at the local, state, or national level controls every activity.

The left (Democrat) favors more government to provide services, which translates into fewer opportunities for capital and tighter control on individual and business behavior.

 The right (Republican) favors less government, greater capital opportunities, and more personal freedoms. Unconstrained, the result is the exploitation of the environment and labor.

A cynic would state it differently. Both sides are greedy - the far left for power and control, the far right for power and money. The political extreme of both sides is essentially the same, an authoritarian government.

Throughout America's short history, the conflict between too much or too little government repeats itself with a pendulum effect, but has largely remained within the range required for a free people living in an opportunity driven system.

On the chart, the band in the middle is labeled "the opportunity zone', the sweet spot between needed regulation and the freedoms required to promote entrepreneurship and enjoy liberty. An opportunity driven society finds the right balance between capital, freedoms, social needs, and the environment.

The chart indicates the U.S. is moving out of the opportunity zone and towards an authoritarian state. Reviewing the economic data for the last six years verifies the effect. The Obama administration takes an extreme position, endangering capital and freedoms, and setting the stage for further deviation from a balanced society.

Most Americans, regardless of political labels, share values that are more centrist, well within the sweet range where businesses and the people flourish. We care about each other, education, personal safety, the rule of law and freedoms. It is convenient for politicians to divide us when possible, but we must remember elected officials work for us. We want businesses to be profitable and create jobs, but reject exploitation by a bloated Wall Street.

We need the free-market principles of capitalism to drive an economic system capable of providing all the goods and services required by a modern society, and the education, health care systems and infrastructure to support it.

The only hope for the future of the entire world population depends upon the constructive application of science and technology, and true respect for planet earth.

An Action Agenda

The current administration is on an obsessive mission, and the rest of the country has not even defined a collective direction.

Ideally, Americans will agree on a shared vision and mission. It would be useful if industry, education, science, and healthcare, performed a needs assessment, then worked with the people developing options. Given the nature of the Internet, all of this is possible, and the people can participate in the definition of an inclusive "greater good," containing a national mission. As consultants, we call the process due diligence. The results would provide guidance to the legislators, who need to step back, reassess the situation, and synchronize with the people.

The rebirth of America rests with restoring the freedoms to a free market driven, opportunity-based society where entrepreneurs can build new businesses and create jobs in environmentally responsible factories and facilities. Our abundant energy, unlocked, will fuel the most productive and ecologically friendly production system in the world. As a result, the total size of the economic pie will grow larger, providing resources to recharge science, education, and health care. Most of all, it will provide opportunities for current and future generations.

The United States is the only country on earth with all the resources to lead the way into the Fourth Industrial Revolution and the prosperity it will bring to America and the world. With Canada as a partner, it has the potential to become the greatest force for good.

With a new vision of a society based on entrepreneurship, responsibility, environmental stewardship, and freedom for all, America will once again be competitive, the land of the free, the home of brave, and there will be opportunities for all.

America's better days are ahead. While God gave us the resources, it is up to us to use them wisely and morally.

160

About the Author

Wayne Staley established Affinity Systems LLC, a system consulting company, in 1997.

 An Army veteran and military Operating Room Technician, Wayne was the NCOIC for his surgical unit. While attending college, he worked as an ER and X-Ray Technician.

Educated in computer technology, business, and manufacturing systems, he has managed Corporate Information Technology, Materials, Logistics, and manufacturing.

He was Manager of Shop Operations for a complex fabrication facility, including a foundry, machine shop, metal punching and forming, annealing, aluminum die-casting/injection, metal forming, and welding. Wayne worked on integrated supply chain programs with China based suppliers, and collaboration programs with Dow Chemical and other customers, developing processes and new products. He performed numerous studies on energy, products, and doing business in Mexico. He is NAFTA certified. He served for eleven years on the City/County information processing commission, the last year as Chairperson.

He has managed numerous Business Strategy, Enterprise Resource Planning (ERP), and process improvement projects (VMP) in manufacturing, government, distribution, and convention management.

He developed training materials for ERP, Supply-Chain Management, Strategy, and Process Improvement. He created Phase Four Graphics LLC, a graphic arts company, phasefourgraphics.com, and CompetitiveAmerica.us, advocating for American industry. A frequent speaker at APICS and AITP meetings, conferences and seminars, he is the author of six books.

ERP Information at the Speed of Reality

Wayne L Staley

Information reality

Every type of business must execute effectively and move from a physical and information reality of weeks and days to minutes and seconds. The smart enterprise builds intelligence gathering in near real time, taking full advantage of faster operations.

The games people play

Consultants, executives, project leaders, software suppliers all play games that introduce unnecessary variables into a complex process. We share our experience of forty-five years because it will help businesses to succeed. Some stories are enlightening, but not funny because companies, their employees, and ownership paid the price.

Due diligence

Ignorance is not bliss, excusable or acceptable. Discover the truth – think beyond the obvious and overcome ignorance with education and training. Major project pitfalls are assumptions, bias, and fixation.

Assemble the puzzle

ERP projects are complex, involving strategies, internal assessments, evaluation of multiple alternatives, and making critical business decisions. They require assigning high performers to project teams, taking them away from important daily activities. ERP systems are so expensive that failure is not an option. Evidence based decisions and a structured process lead to successful results.

ERP Lessons Learned-Structured Process

Wayne L Staley

ERP Lessons Learned - Structured Process Is an expanded software selection and Implementation process extracted from ERP Information at the Speed of Reality.

ERP projects are tough work but very important for the future of your company. Competitive pressures will only intensify, and companies will compete at ever-faster speeds.

Those serving as project team members, directly or on functional teams, hold the operational effectiveness of your employer in your hands.

As you take actions to get the job done, the outcome will affect many lives.

Never let your guard down and stay alert. Situations will not always reflect reality. Ask tough questions and demand answers from software suppliers, each other, and fellow workers. Quality is important. Establish high goals and challenge yourself and others to achieve the standards. When the project is complete, and people are working with the results, all will celebrate having done the project correctly.

To everyone in the organization - a successful project result is a positive for you and fellow workers. You will grow in knowledge and importance to your current and perhaps future organization.

Pathway to Adaptability

Wayne L Staley

"If you don't know where you're going, any path will take you there."

The Cheshire cat

Alice's Wonderland is a labyrinth filled with strange places, unusual ideas, unexpected occupants, and unpredictable events. One danger is running ever faster but staying in the same place, a clear sign of lost direction.

This description applies to the real business world but even more volatile and unforgiving forces' sort it all out – the marketplace. It demands the correct products, appropriately priced and available now.

Speed is King!

Pathway to Adaptability is for corporate leaders, executives, managers, and administrators who govern businesses of all types.

In Pathway to Adaptability, you will travel on an eight-step pathway through the corporate alignment process. The book provides assessments to track your progress.

Enterprises must become very smart, building real-time intelligence into every activity. Without accurate information foundations, and process improvement, adaptability is not achievable and significant opportunities will be lost.

"This book has invaluable information on LEAN Six Sigma Methodology that is used in my company, and has been used as a reference point in many of our LEAN Focus Groups across the country. I highly recommend Wayne Staley's book." Amazon review by Black Belt.

Productivity Prescriptions for Health Care

Wayne L Staley and Jon Bingol

The primary mission of health care professionals, executive leadership, and associates is delivering quality health care to patients. The past model was doctor/ patient, but numerous new wedges were driven between the two, adding complexity and cost.

The ACA, passed in 2010, created a new health care model, and transformation is proving difficult and expensive. Compliance puts many health care organizations in a financial bind. One of the most powerful tools to address operational problems is process improvement programs.

Crunch Time for Health Care, written before the resolution of sundry challenges to the ACA, contained discussions regarding the viability and implications of the law. With the issues settled and Health care focused on compliance, a refreshed manuscript was required.

Productivity Prescriptions for Health Care provides a structured program methodology for defining and implementing contemporary programs specifically designed for the special requirements of health care organizations.

To the practitioners of Lean, Health care is a special calling. Nothing parallels the heart-breaking experience of watching life fade while working frantically to preserve it. The thought that process improvement potentially makes life saving tools less accessible, is repugnant and immoral. We have created a special symbol as a constant reminder, life trumps efficiency.

Productivity improvement programs are required for future Health care sustainability, with quality and efficiency the twins for success.

Crunch Time for Health Care

Wayne L Staley and Jon Bingol

Continuous Process Improvement
for the Medical Profession

CRUNCH TIME For Health Care

People are the competitive advantage

H-LEAN

Wayne Staley and Jon Bingol

Time is running out for health care, as we know it

Dramatic changes in the health care system are causing paradigm shifts in patient care. While the intent was to improve quality, the cost of medical care is still unchecked and profitability is suffering.

Time is life

Medical care must embrace patient-centered process improvement such as reducing the "door to balloon" time. An example is moving the 12 lead EKG from the emergency room to the ambulance, allowing the patient to go directly to the cath lab.

Current and future patients need this information to help them make informed medical decisions in the new world of healthcare.

Time is Money

H-Lean is a concept designed around health care. Every person in the industry will be involved in or affected by the dramatic changes. This book will help you become more knowledgeable, allowing you to participate through positive ACTION.

BIBLIOGRAPHY

The Evolutionary Entrepreneur-Beyond the Passion

Mark Burwell

Lateral Thinking for Management   Edward de Bono

Future Jobs- Solving the Employment and Skill Crisis

Edward E. Gordon

The 2010 Meltdown   Edward E. Gordon

Thriving on Chaos   Tom Peters

Complex Organizations   Amitai Etzioni

The Change Agent   Lee Grossman

Consilience: The Unity of Knowledge   Edward O. Wilson

Performance Consulting : Moving Beyond Training

Dana Gaines Robinson

James C. Robinson

Complexity – The Emerging Science at the Edge of Order and Chaos

M. Mitchell Waldrop

Leadership and the New Science: Learning about Organization from an Orderly Universe   Margaret J. Wheatley

Successful Management by Objectives   Karl Albrecht

Liberation Management   Tom Peters

The Machine That Changed the World   James Womak

Daniel Jones

Daniel Roos

The 13 Secrets of Power Performance   Roger Dawson

Value Migration   Adrian J. Slywotzky

The Mind of the Strategist   Kenichi Ohmae

The Rise and Fall of Strategic Planning   Henry Mintzberg

The Fifth Discipline: The Art and Practice of the Learning Organization

Peter Senge

The 7 Habits of Highly Effective People   Stephen R. Covey

The New Rules   John P. Cotter

Leading Change   John P. Cotter

Crossing the Chasm   Geoffrey A. Moore

Atlas Shrugged   Ayn Rand

Top Management Strategy What it is and How to Make It Work

Benjamin B. Tregoe

John W. Zimmerman

The Theory of Inventive Problem Solving   www.mazur.net/triz/
40 Principles-TRIZ Keys to Technical Innovation
Genrich Atschuller

One Minute Manager   Kenneth Blanchard, PhD
                                            Spencer Johnson, MD
To Err is Human: Building a Safer Health System
                                            Institute of Medicine
MRPII Unlocking America's Productivity Potential
                                            Oliver W. Wight
What the CEO Wants You to Know   Ram Charan
High Velocity Leadership   Brian K. Muirhead
                                            William L. Simon
Lean Thinking   James P. Womack
                                            Daniel T. Jones
The Frontiers of Management   Peter Drucker
The Handbook of Strategic Expertise   Catherine Hayden
Quality is Free   Philip B. Crosby
Kanban – Just In Time at Toyota Edited by Japan Management
                                            Association
The Japanese Art of War   Thomas Cleary
It's Not Luck   Eliyahu M. Goldratt
Bionomics: Economy as Ecosystem   Michael Rothschild
Business at the Speed of Thought   Bill Gates
Theory of Constraints   Eliyahu M. Goldratt
The Goal   Eliyahu M. Goldratt
                                            Jeff Cox
How to Manage Change Effectively   Donald L. Kirkpatrick
Technology, Management and Society   Peter F. Drucker
Lightning Strategies for Innovation   Willard L. Zangwill
CRM At The Speed of Light   Paul Greenberg
The Reengineering Revolution   Michael Hammer
Beyond Reengineering   Michael Hammer
World Class Manufacturing: The Lessons of Simplicity Applied
                                            Richard J. Schonberger
Computer Applications in Manufacturing
                                            Thomas G. Gunn
Best Practices : Building Your Business With Customer Focused Solution
                                            Robert Hiebeler
                                            Thomas B. Kelly
                                            Charles Ketterman

Solving Business Problems by Simulation

> Jan Szymankiewicz
> James McDonald
> Keith Turner

Customer Centered Growth-Five Strategies for Building Competitive Advantage

> Richard Whiteley
> Diane Hessan

Inside Teams – How 20 World-Class Organizations are Winning Through Teamwork

> Richard S. Wellins
> William C. Byham
> George R. Dixon

Supply Chain Development for the Lean Enterprise

> Robin Cooper
> Regine Slagmulder

The Concept of Corporate Strategy   Kenneth R. Andrews

Complexity and the Experience of Leading Organizations

> Edited By Douglas Griffin
> Ralph Stacey

The Art of Innovation   Tom Kelly

> Jonathan Littman

Principle Centered Leadership   Steven R. Covey

Breakthrough Thinking: The Seven Principles of Creative Problem Solving

> Gerald Nader, PhD
> Shozo Hibini, PhD
> John Farrell

Great Leaders Grow: Becoming A Leader for Life

> Kenneth Blanchard
> Mark MIller

Systematic Innovation: An Introduction to Triz

> John Terninko
> Alla Zusman
> Boris Zlotin

The Audacity of Hope: Thoughts on Reclaiming the American Dream

> Barack Obama

Silent Spring   Rachel Carson

Mein Kampf   Adolf Hitler

Goebbels' Principles of Propaganda   Leonard W. Doob

I Am Malala: The Girl Who Stood Up for Education and Was Shot by the Taliban

> Malala Yousafzai
> Christina Lamb

Infidel   Ayaan Hirsi Ali
The Jihadis Return: ISIS and the New Sunni Uprising
                                                         Patrick Cockburn
Lying Cheating Scum   Ed Uravic
Duty: Memoirs of a Secretary of War   Robert M. Gates
Worthy Fights: A Memoir of Leadership in War and Peace
                                                         Leon Panetta
An Essay on the Principle of Population   Thomas Robert Malthus
The Limits to Growth – A Report for the Club of Rome's Project on the
 Predicament of Mankind   Donella H. Meadows
                                                         Dennis L. Meadows
                                                         Jorgen Randers
                                                         William W. Behrens III
Understanding ICD-10 and ICD-10-PC   Mary Jo Bowie
                                                         Regina Schaffer
Nineteen Eighty-Four   George Orwell
Two Intellectual Systems: Matter-energy and the Monetary Culture
                                                         M. King Hubbert
A Theory of Human Motivation   Abraham Maslow
Stonewalled: My Fight for Truth Against the Forces of Obstruction,
Intimidation, and Harassment in Obama's Washington
                                                         Sharyl Attkisson
The Trial   Franz Kafka
Brave New World   Aldous Huxley
I, Robot   Isaac Asimov
Fahrenheit 451   Ray Bradbury
Do Androids Dream of Electric Sheep?   Phillip K. Dick
The Handmaid's Tale   Margaret Atwood
Parable of the Sower   Octavia E. Butler
War and Anti-War - Survival at the Dawn of the 21st Century
                                                         Alvin and Heidi Toffler
The Art of Innovation   Tom Kelley
                                                         Jonathan Littman
The Garden Earth - The Case for Ecological Morality
                                                         Bruce Allsopp
Natural Capitalism - Creating The Next Industrial Revolution
                                                         Paul Hawken
                                                         Amory Lovins
                                                         L Hunter Lovins
A Contract with the Earth   Newt Gingrich

Terry L Maple
Soil Not Oil - Environmental Justice in a Time of Climate Crisis
Vandana Shiva
Towards some operational principles of sustainable development
Herman E. Daly
American Bombing of Libya: An International Legal Analysis
Gregory Francis Intoccia
Terrorism in North Africa: Before and After Benghazi
Daniel Byman
Under Fire: The Untold Story of the Attack in Benghazi
Fred Burton
Samuel M. Katz
Rules for Radicals: A Practical Primer for Realistic Radicals
Saul D. Alinski

Whitepapers and presentations

Affordable Care Act
www.business.gov/law/full
Increasing Returns and the New World of Business
Brian Arthur
From Fragmentation to Integration: Building Learning Communities
www.pegasuscom.com
Why the Pursuit of Innovation Usually Fails Adam Hartung
Five Discovery Skills that Distinguish Great Innovators
Jeff DyerHal Gergersen
Clayton M. Christensen
Goals in Effective Communications and Public Speaking
John Eric Staley
Lessons Not Learned About Innovation   Sean Silverthorne
Innovate the Steve Jobs Way   Carmine Gallo
Know Your Brain   www.ninds.nih.gov
Rewire Your Brain for Success   Gene Anger
Quality Performance   Dow Chemical
A Disruptive Solution for Business   Advanced Leadership Inst
Harvard University
Clayton M. Christensen
Skills of Successful Entrepreneurs   Arlen Meyers

Five Key Trends in Business Technology   Christina Orlovsky
Why Accountable Care Organizations Won't Deliver Better Business – And
market Innovation Will   Rita Numerof, Ph.D.
On the Mend - Revolutionizing Health Care
                                           John Toussaint, MD
                                           Roger A. Gerard, PhD
                                           Emily Adams
Breaking Business Research: "Accountable Care" Unlikely
                                           Margot Crouch
The Inglehart-Weizel Cultural Map of the World
                                           Ronald Inglehart
                                           Christian Welzel
The Power of Personal Values   Rov Posner
Radically Rethinking Business Delivery   Jim Champy
Innovation in Business Delivery Systems: A Conceptual Framework
                                           Vincent K. Omachonu
                                           Norman G. Einspruch
DATT (Direction Attention Thinking Tools) Edward Bono
Introduction to Basic I-TRIZ   www.ideationtriz.com
Forms of Social organization and Leadership – Insights into individuals and
complex organizations   J.K. Hazy
Surprise and Anticipation: The Principles of War as Applied to Business
                                           Chet Richards
Six Sigma   Motorola
ST Morphology   ECGpedia
Group Techniques for Program Planning
                                           Andre L. Delbecq
                                           A. H. Van de Ven
                                           David H. Gustafson
New Leadership Thinking in Play – Simulation Develops Leadership
                                           Catherine J. Rezak
                                           Kathleen Hurson
An Integrated Planning Model in Business: From Vision to Reality
                                           Carrie Hout
Blurring Manufacturing and Service Boundaries
                                           William T. Walker
                                           Richard E. Crandell, PhD
Adverse Events in Businesss: National Incidence among Medicare
Aseptic Technique   www.infectioncontrol.com
Electrocardiography – Understanding the EKG Waveform

John Quinn

Improving Emergency Department Flow Through The RME

Michele Hoover

Santiago Duarte

Lory Wallach

Effective Thinking   Bono

Parallel Thinking   Guy Blelloch

A3 Thinking and Standardized Work   Art Smalley

Managing Dynamic Complexity: The Foundation of TPS

Paul H. Pittman, PhD

J. Brian Atwater, PhD

The Economics and Politics of Climate Change an Appeal to Reason

Nigel Lawson

The Factory of the Future -A practical guide to harnessing new value in manufacturing   Zebra Technologies

The Tragedy of Our Time   Peter Senge

Redistribution, Inequality, and Growth

Jonathan D. Ostry

Andrew Berg

Charalambos G. Tsangarides

A Redistribution of Wealth: A moral issue

Dan Kellar,

The New Religion of Eco-Fundamentalism?

The Globalist

Fairness and Redistribution: US versus Europe*

Alberto Alesina

George-Marios Angeletos

Using Location Intelligence to Maximize the Value of BI

Esri.com

Big Data: he Next Frontier for Innovation, Competition, and Productivity

McKinsey Global Institute

Made in America, Again: Why Manufacturing will return to the U.S.

BCG Boston Consulting Group

Barack Obama, Judge of Life or Death   Ben Shapiro

VA Crises Getting Lost in Scandal Overload

Roger Aronoff

What Does Entrepreneurship Really Come Down To? An Interview With Stephen M.R. Covey   Scott Cooney

U.S. Drops to 47th on Press Freedom Index; Annual Press Freedom Index

Reporters Without Borders

174

Obama's 'Operation Choke Point' Seeks to Destroy Sectors of Private Lending Industry   Michael Patrick Leahy
Private Companies Mimic Government's 'Choke Point' Program
                                    Rusty Weiss
Judicial Watch Sues DOJ for Operation Choke Point Records
                                    Judicial Watch
Benghazi attack could have been prevented if US hadn't 'switched sides in the War on Terror' and allowed $500 MILLION of weapons to reach al-Qaeda militants, reveals damning report
                                    David Martosko
Email Shows Adviser Urged Rice to Blame Video for Benghazi Attack
                                    Melanie Batley
Inhofe: Benghazi 'Worst of All Cover-ups'
                                    Todd Beamon
Material Support to Terrorism: The Case of Libya
                                    Clare Lopez
Media Hits and Misses Covering Benghazi Press Conference
                                    Roger Aronoff
Report: Ex-CIA Deputy Director May Have Altered Benghazi Talking Points
                                    Michael Morell
Benghazi's Tough Questions   Daniel Greenfield

URLS

ArcGIS Platform - Innovation through Geography
        Http://www.esri.com/software/arcgis
Pew Forum on Religion & Public Life / U.S. Religious Landscape Survey
Costhelper.com
Jodi Jacobson, Editor-in-Chief/RH RealityCheck,
http://www.politico.com/story/2014/01/contraceptive-mandate-obamacare-little-sisters-for-the-poor-supreme-court-102587.html
http://www.historylearningsite.co.uk/propaganda_in_nazi_germany
Holocaust Timeline: The Rise of the Nazi Party
fcit.coedu.usf.edu/holocaust/timeline/nazirise.htm
http://feedingamerica.org/.
www.wkrn.com/story/21858334/study-finds-teachers...pocket-on-supplies
http://www.huffingtonpost.com/2012/08/23/survey-many-teachers-repo_n_1822777.html

http://redalertpolitics.com/2014/11/10/obamacare-architect-jonathan-gruber-law-passed-thanks-lack-transparency/#ZHpDjlUrwp8Jb8Fx.99

http://reason.com/blog/2014/07/24/watch-obamacare-architect-jonathan-gruber

http://www.nejm.org/doi/full/10.1056/NEJMp1403294

Chicago Booth/Kellogg School Financial Trust Index

Harvard University's Institute of Politics

The Declaration of Independence

The Bill of Rights

Presidential Oath of Office, Military Officers, Enlisted Personnel

Article II Section 2 of the U.S. Constitution

http://jonathanturley.files.wordpress.com/

http://newsbusters.org/blogs/melissa-mullins/2014/10/31/usa-todays-susan-page-obama-team-most-dangerous-press-us-history#sthash.aViAStJK.dpuf

http://www.hubbertpeak.com/hubbert/1956/1956.pdf

Love Canal and Its Mixed Legacy

http://www.nytimes.com/2013/11/25/booming/love-canal-and-its-mixed-legacy.html

http://variety.com/2014/film/news/hackers-threaten-sony-employees-in-new-email-your-family-will-be-in-danger-1201372230/

http://www.pbs.org/newshour/bb/science-jan-june11-databreach_04-27/

http://variety.com/2014/film/news/sony-hack-unparalleled-cyber-security-firm-1201372889/Sony *Hack*

http://online.wsj.com/articles/sony-pictures-hack-reveals-more-data-than-previously-believed-1417734425

http://www.csoonline.com/article/2130877/data-protection/the-15-worst-data-security-breaches-of-the-21st-century.html

http://townhall.com/columnists/johnhawkins/

http://www.chron.com/news/nation-world/nation/article/Americans

http://www.judicialwatch.org/press-room/press-releases/judicial-watch-sues-doj-operation-choke-point-records/